THE CROSS

THE CROSS

Saved by the Shame of It All

Chris Altrock

COLLEGE PRESS
PUBLISHING COMPANY
Joplin, Missouri

Illustration and Cover Design by Mark A. Cole

Library of Congress Cataloging-in-Publication Data

Altrock, Chris, 1968–
    The cross: saved by the shame of it all / Chris Altrock.
      p.   cm.
    Includes bibliographical references.
    ISBN 0-89900-805-4 (paperback)
    1. Jesus Christ—Crucifixion.   2. Christian life—
Churches of Christ authors.   I. Title.
BT453.A48 1998
232.96'3—dc21
                                          98-3459
                                          CIP

Dedicated To:

Gary Cox,
who first told me about the cross;

Allen Black and Rick Oster,
who showed me how to study the cross;

Harold Shank,
who exemplifies the proclamation of the cross;

The University Church of Christ,
which allows me to preach the cross;

Kendra my wife,
who has loved me for eight years
in spite of my failures to live a life worthy of the cross.

Thanks To:

Larry Linley,
for reading much of this manuscript and offering
advice concerning its content and style;

Harding University Graduate School of Religion librarians,
for helping me locate original sources.

TABLE OF CONTENTS

THE CROSS

Part One

Part One

Recovering the Relevancy of the Cross

In the late 1800's, artist William Holman Hunt and his new bride Fanny Waugh packed their hopes and their house and moved to Florence, Italy. The romance of Europe was to be the backdrop against which the couple forged their bonds of love. Soon the giddy joy of marriage gave birth to a son. But puerperal fever brought the baby's life, and the couple's dreams, to a premature end. Grief drove the childless couple from Florence, the city of romance, to Jerusalem, the city of religion. There William's wounds healed and he renewed his painting career. Fanny, however, never recovered from her grief. Six months later she joined her son in death.

During this time of tragedy and loss, William painted one of his most striking pieces. It was a somber painting reflective of the pain which he had recently endured. The painting depicted the imminent death of an individual. Even its title suggested the mournful context in which it was painted. The painting was called "The Shadow of Death."

It portrayed a young Jesus in his early twenties working in his father's carpentry shop. Moments before, Jesus had been sawing a piece of wood. Now he was standing, as if to rest. The saw remained stuck halfway through the piece of wood. As Jesus stretched, his head tilted toward the ceiling and his arms thrust toward the walls.

On the floor, a woman knelt — probably Mary — with her back to the viewer. She had been peering into an open chest in which a crown was visible. The crown, a gift from the Magi, may have reminded Mary of her royal dreams for Jesus. But her dreams were now shattered by the image created by her son's shadow against the workshop wall.

The shadow fell across a tool rack fastened on the wall behind Jesus. The rack resembled a cross bar, its sharp tools acting like spikes. And as the horizontal shape of the tool rack crashed into the vertical shadow of Jesus, the shape of a cross filled the workshop.[1]

"The Shadow of Death" portrays the centrality of the cross in the life of Christ. Even in the midst of another day in the workshop, the cross was close. It peered around the corner. It made its presence known. Hunt's painting suggests that the cross stands at the center of Jesus' entire life.

Yet the painting also seems to suggest that the cross should stand at the center of our lives. Something about a two-thousand-year-old cross enabled Hunt to successfully swim his river of grief. Something about Jesus' timbers allowed Hunt to make sense of senseless death. Something about it gave him strength to live when he wanted to die. Hunt's painting seems to suggest that the cross should stand at the center of our lives, as it did in his. The cross alone has what we need to weather life's storms. The cross alone has what we want to live successfully in spite of our circumstances.

Yet for many today, the cross makes no sense. Some see it as an ancient relic. This view of the cross is exemplified by the comment of a San Francisco worshiper recorded in a 1990 *Newsweek*. The mother of a four-year-old child remarked that she figured it was time to get serious about God when her daughter pointed to a crucifix and asked "What's that man doing, Mom?"[2] In the midst of grinding schedules, relationship struggles, and spiritual confusion, many are asking that four-year-old's question. What *does* that man's dated actions on the cross have to do with my life today? Some see the cross as an ancient relic.

Others see the cross as a cheap religious symbol. The April 1995 edition of *The New Yorker* caricatured an Easter Bunny in a business suit crucified on a 1040A Tax Form. The magazine communicated what many now believe: Easter is a time for remembering the demands of the government, not the death and resurrection of Jesus. The cross has been cheapened and trivialized. Few understand what took place at Golgotha, much less its implications for modern living. Many see the cross as just a cheap religious symbol.

In 1995 I witnessed the irrelevancy of the cross first hand when I served on a building campaign in Chihuahua City, Mexico. Three van loads of teenagers and adults hit the city with hammers and hearts to help two local churches. The middle of the laborious week was broken by a short trip south to Cuatehmoc — a colorful village nestled in a quiet green valley. Two spots in Cuatehmoc served as focal points of the trip. One was an ancient cathedral. The other was the outdoor "mercado" — a local shopping strip. Both spots offered unexpected commentaries on the cross.

The cathedral was as full of silence as it was empty of worshipers. The dusty stained-glass windows and dark wood pews absorbed all sound. A replica of the cross hung at the back of the marble-floored auditorium. Cherry-colored blood dripped from it. A mouth opened in a frozen agony. Empty eyes stared upward. The cross was draped in shadows and encased in a glass cage to protect it from vandals.

The mercado, on the other hand, was as full of people as it was empty of silence. Dark-haired farmers picked over produce. Multicolored rugs hung in narrow halls. Loud accordions played on battery operated radios. And vendor after vendor beckoned in broken English for us to spend our money at his table.

One table in particular displayed reproductions of the crucifixion. A plastic Jesus hung on a plastic cross, its edges rough from the seams of the mold, its paint barely covering the orange hue of the plastic. Other trinkets kept the cross company. A red plastic sports car lay to the right. An imitation Barbie doll stood to the left. The cross was a cheap trinket among a sea of trinkets.

Both the cathedral and the mercado offered modern commentaries on the cross. In one the cross was an object to be observed. In the other, it was a product to be purchased. In one the cross was a timeworn relic. In the other it was a tinseltown toy. In both the cross had lost all relevancy to real life. It was too ancient to carry meaning for the modern world. It was too cheap to offer solutions for our complex lives.

Yet Hunt's lonely portrait of the cross remains. Its message still sounds: the cross must stand at the center of our lives. Not only is the cross relevant to living, it is the only thing which can make life worth living. That's what this book is about. It argues that far from being an ancient relic or a cheap religious symbol, the cross is the most relevant symbol for modern society.

Specifically, the cross shows us how to live: how to live with God and how to live with others. It is these areas of living which cause most of us our greatest confusion. We want to know how to live with family, friends, or coworkers. Thus we hunger for literature like *The Book of Virtues* and *The Moral Compass* by William Bennett which illustrate how to treat others. We mourn the loss of morals which once guided us like beacons along the dark path of relationships. We sympathize with statements like Jonathan Alter's: ". . . millions of American kids are growing up without a moral compass."[3] We want to know how to be a more sensitive spouse. We want to raise good kids. We hope to treat that annoying coworker with compassion and patience. We long to know how to live with others.

We also long to know how to live with God. We nod in agreement with novelist Reynold Price's statement that there is one sentence all humankind craves to hear:

"The maker of all things loves and wants me."[4] We want to understand how much God loves and how much God wants.

The cross is the single answer to those questions. In biblical terms, questions about living with others and living with God are couched in the vocabulary of "grace" and "discipleship." Grace deals with God's love for us and our love for others. Discipleship deals with our responsibility toward God and toward others. The cross illuminates these issues in an unparalleled way. It is a paradigm for living with God and with neighbor.

And one aspect of the cross empowers it to be such a relevant paradigm — its disgrace. The disgrace of the cross justifies placing the cross in the center of our lives. The disgrace of the cross answers our most haunting questions of life with others and life with God:

How do I move from simply enduring marriage to really enjoying marriage?

How can I treat my neighbor with love when his dog scares my kids and his house lowers my property value?

How can I face God when my hands are stained with sin?

How can I live with stability in a society which is becoming more and more unstable?

This book explores how the cross's disgrace answers such questions. In the first section, we'll look at the cross from a perspective you probably haven't seen before. We won't explore the anatomy of the death caused by the cross, or the specific methods of crucifixion. Lengthy books have already been written on those aspects of the cross. Instead, we will explore the disgrace of the cross. Uncovering that ancient disgrace, we'll recapture its relevancy to and centrality in our lives. Once the disgraceful image of the cross is fixed indelibly in our minds, we'll be ready to explore its implications for living with God and with others, which make up parts two and three of the book. And finally, having been comforted and challenged by the cross's paradigm for living, we'll spend some quiet time in the fourth and final part of the book simply reflecting on the cross. Right now, let's proceed. Let's explore the vast caverns of the cross and witness afresh its ancient disgrace and its modern relevancy for living.

Endnotes

1. Raymond Watkinson, *Pre-Raphaelite Art and Design* (Greenwich, CT: New York Graphic Society Ltd., 1970) #35; I was first made aware of this painting by John Stott, *The Cross of Christ* (Downers Grove, IL: InterVarsity Press, 1986), 17.

2. *Newsweek* (December 17, 1990).

3. Jonathan Alter, "What Works: Build a Sense of Character," *Newsweek* (May 19, 1995).

4. Quoted by Philip Yancy in *Christianity Today* (November 23, 1993): 22.

Study Questions

1. Has the cross of Christ ever been a source of strength or recovery for you in the way it seems to have been for William Holman Hunt? Explain.

2. Can you think of other illustrations in modern society which show that, for many, the cross is simply an ancient relic? Has the ancient nature of the cross ever caused you to struggle with its relevancy? Explain.

3. In what other ways has society cheapened and trivialized the cross? Share a situation or a time in life when the cross was just a cheap religious symbol to you.

4. This book deals with two major areas of our lives: how to live with others, and how to live with God. What are some of your recent struggles in the area of trying to live with others?

5. Share a recent time in which you struggled to live with God.

6. In what area, living with others, or living with God, do you experience more struggles? What

other paradigms (standards, models, etc.) besides
the cross have you used in trying to effectively
answer questions which have to do with living
with others or living with God?

† 1 †

The First Century Cross and the Twentieth Century Veil

Centering on the Cross

What William Holman Hunt painted with brushes, Jesus painted with words. Just as the cross was central to Hunt's painting, so it was central to Jesus' preaching. Throughout his ministry, Jesus equated his identity as the Christ with his mission on the cross. The two were inseparable. To understand Jesus as the Christ, you must accept his mission on the cross. Jesus made that clear to his closest followers in Luke 9:18-22:

> Once when Jesus was praying in private and his disciples were with him, he asked them, "Who do the crowds say I am?" They replied, "Some say John the Baptist; others say Elijah; and still others, that one of the prophets of long ago has come back to life." "But what about you?" he asked. "Who do you say I am?" Peter answered, "The Christ of God." Jesus strictly warned them not to tell this to anyone. And he said, "The Son of

> Man must suffer many things and be rejected by the elders, chief priests and teachers of the law, and he must be killed and on the third day be raised to life."

Peter gave the correct answer to Jesus' multiple choice test. Jesus was not John the Baptist. He was not Elijah. And he was not one of the prophets come back to life. Jesus was the Christ of God.

Yet Jesus took Peter's positive answer and put a negative spin on it. According to Jesus, to understand what it meant to be the Christ, one had to understand what it meant to die on a cross. To "be killed and on the third day be raised to life" defined an essential characteristic of the Christ's identity. The Christ and his cross were synonymous.

Not only did Jesus erect the cross as the central theme of his life, so did his followers. Of all the possible topics Peter could have preached after the death, resurrection, and ascension of Jesus, Peter preached about the cross:

> Men of Israel, listen to this: Jesus of Nazareth was a man accredited by God to you by miracles, wonders and signs, which God did among you through him, as you yourselves know. This man was handed over to you by God's set purpose and foreknowledge; and you, with the help of wicked men, put him to death by nailing him to the cross. . . . God has made this Jesus, whom you crucified, both Lord and Christ (Acts 2:22-23,36).

Years later, after countless sermons to countless crowds, another Christ-follower named Paul summarized his own preaching in this way:

For what I received I passed on to you as of first importance: that Christ died for our sins according to the Scriptures, that he was buried, that he was raised on the third day according to the Scriptures, and that he appeared to Peter, and then to the Twelve (1 Cor 15:3-5).

At the beginning of the same letter, Paul summarized his message even further: "For the message of the cross is foolishness to those who are perishing, but to us who are being saved it is the power of God" (1 Cor 1:18).

The "message of the cross" is what Paul preached. In fact, while he was with the Corinthians, Paul claimed to have focused only on the cross: "For I resolved to know nothing while I was with you except Jesus Christ and him crucified" (1 Cor 2:2).

For Jesus' followers, the cross stood at the center of their thinking and their living. Its shadow fell across almost every page of their writings and every day of their actions.

Living *on* the Cross and *under* the Cross

Jesus and his followers centered their works and their words on the cross. More specifically, however, for Jesus and his followers, the cross stood at the center of two of the most important issues in Christianity: grace and discipleship. For them the cross captured everything involved in having salvation *from* God, and having to sacrifice *for* God. The cross summarized what it meant to have something *free* of cost, and what it meant to *count* the cost. It was a paradigm for Christian living. The cross stood at both ends of the continuum between receiving *from* God, and responding *to* God.

The Cross: Saved by the Shame of It All

On one end of that continuum, Jesus brandished the cross to demonstrate the sharp challenge of discipleship: "If anyone would come after me, he must deny himself and take up his cross daily and follow me" (Luke 9:23). Paul also sketched the cross as a symbol for holy living:

> Those who belong to Christ Jesus have crucified the sinful nature with its passions and desires (Gal 5:24).

> Be imitators of God, therefore, as dearly loved children and live a life of love, just as Christ loved us and gave himself up for us as a fragrant offering and sacrifice to God (Eph 5:1-2).

To live *on* the cross was to live a life of service to others and to God. Complete self-sacrifice was demanded by the cross.

On the other end of the continuum, the cross was raised in the face of those who tried to earn life after death: "I do not set aside the grace of God, for if righteousness could be gained through the law, Christ died for nothing" (Gal 2:21)!

In the same letter, Paul erected the cross to condemn those who believed their salvation depended upon their performance:

> You who are trying to be justified by law have been alienated from Christ; you have fallen away from grace. . . . Brothers, if I am still preaching circumcision, why am I still being persecuted? In that case the offense of the cross has been abolished (Gal 5:4,11).

To live *under* the cross was to live a life of celebration. Complete forgiveness and righteousness were given by the cross.

For Jesus and his followers, the cross stood at the center of the two crucial issues of Christian living. It summed up the grandness of grace. It captured the demands of discipleship. When Jesus and his followers wanted to illustrate how to live life as one given everything from God, they pointed to the cross. When they wanted to illustrate how to live life as one willing to give up all for God, they pointed to the cross. The cross was *the* paradigm for living.

In particular, it was the paradigm for learning how to live with others and how to live with God. When people wanted to know how to get along with a cranky spouse, or how to forgive an insenstive coworker, the cross was raised. When people wondered what it would take to gain God's favor, or what God would do when failures of the past crept into the present, the cross was raised. The cross alone provided critical answers to living with others and living with God. Living *on* the cross showed them how to sacrifice for God and for others. Living *under* the cross showed them how to receive mercy from God and how to show mercy to others.

The Disgrace of the Cross

The cross stands at the center. Hunt painted it. Jesus said it. His followers wrote it. But what made the cross the choice of our God, his Son, and his followers? What mark did the cross possess which captured God's attention? Why did a cross become the deathbed for the King of heaven and the symbol for kingdom living?

For some reason, the cross fascinated the Godhead. As the Father gazed across history, his eyes rested on a cross. As the Holy Trio searched for the perfect tool to woo humanity, the cross topped their list. God chose three spikes and two wooden beams over a firing squad or guillotine. The Godhead chose the cross as the one symbol upon which our understanding of grace and discipleship would rest. But why? Why a cross?

One comment, spoken hundreds of years ago, sheds light on this divine choice. A first century historian named Josephus recorded the story of a young Jewish rebel named Eleazar. Eleazar had been taken captive near a Palestinian fortress by a Roman official named Lucilius Bassus. Bassus threatened to crucify Eleazar unless the remaining Jews in the fortress surrendered. According to Josephus, Eleazar then pled for pity. What prompted his pleas is found in the words he used to describe the threatened crucifixion: "[it is] the most pitiable of deaths."[1]

Those ancient words suggest a reason for God's choice of the cross: its pitiable nature. The cross was not unique in the physical pain it produced. The bodies of those devoured by fire on the stake groaned with comparable pain. Nor was the cross unique in its effectiveness. Firing squads and guillotines rarely failed in their objective. Something other than pain and productivity made crucifixion pitiable. Something else elevated it above all other death methods.

What made crucifixion pitiable and thus worthy of the divine choice was this: no other method so brutally and publicly humiliated its victims. John Stott describes it this way in his book *The Cross of Christ*: "It was probably the most cruel method of execution ever practised. . . ."[2]

What made it cruel was not just its physical pain. What made it cruel was also its ability to shame. At its heart, the cross was a tool of public ridicule. Other punishments only stripped the breath from their victims. Crucifixion also stripped honor and dignity. Other methods quickly sucked the life from their victims. Crucifixion slowly humiliated the living to death. It was a method of brutal disgrace. The cross was not chosen by God just because of its ability to cause death. It was chosen because of its ablity to cause disgrace.

That aspect led early followers of God to call the cross a curse:

> If a man guilty of a capital offense is put to death and his body is hung on a tree, you must not leave his body on the tree overnight. Be sure to bury him that same day, because anyone who is hung on a tree is under God's curse (Deut 21:22-23).

The shame of the cross led later scoffers of God to call the cross foolish: "For the message of the cross is foolishness to those who are perishing, but to us who are being saved it is the power of God" (1 Cor 1:18).[3]

When God chose the cross to demonstrate his love, he chose the greatest tool of disgrace. When Jesus and Paul lifted the cross as the paradigm for living, they lifted a symbol dripping with offensiveness.

Disgraceful.	Dishonorable.
Infamous.	Shameful.
Degrading.	Humiliating.

These words strain to define the cross. The amazing disgrace of the cross made it the most appropriate tool for the display of God's amazing grace. The shame of it all makes it the most challenging symbol for modern living.

The Modern Veil

Unfortunately, we no longer understand the disgrace of the cross. There are many things we do understand about crosses and crucifixion. First, from the second to third century AD until today, Christians have sketched the cross and worn the cross to represent their faith.[4] Thus, the shape of the cross is perhaps one the most universally recognized shapes. Second, over the centuries, well over 50 separate hymns have been written about the cross. From "Alas! And Did My Savior Bleed" by Isaac Watts to "The Old Rugged Cross" by George Bennard, our hymnbooks spill notes about the cross.[5] Third, archaeological remains allow us to dissect the cross. In June 1968, a construction crew stumbled into ancient burial chambers in Israel. One of the tombs contained parts of the skeleton of a man who had been crucified in AD 7.[6]

Because of these things, we understand a great deal about the cross. We know its physical shape. We sing its results. We fathom its inner workings. But we no longer know its disgrace. In spite of all we do know about crosses, we don't know its amazing disgrace. A two-thousand-year-old veil covers the vile nature of the cross. Its stench is diluted by time. Its shock is dulled by years. We know the cross only as a tool of execution, not as a tool of embarassment. The veil of time has blanketed the indignity of the cross.

And the veil is thickened by the fact that our culture no longer humiliates people. Our protection from disgraceful treatment is a constitutional right. We are guaranteed immunity from cruel and unusual punishment. As a result, we have no modern parallel to the cross.

Recent events in the American legal system illustrate just how far removed we are from the experience of crucifixion. In May 1994, John Wayne Gacy faced execution by lethal injection at the Stateville penitentiary in Joliet, Illinois. The procedure normally lasts five minutes. But Gacy took eighteen minutes to die. A clog in the delivery tube attached to his arm prevented the lethal prescription from entering his bloodstream quickly enough. Gacy snorted just before death-chamber attendants pulled a curtain around him as they struggled to clear the tube. His less than graceful death drew rounds of protests.

On Sept. 2, 1983, Jimmy Lee Gray entered the gas chamber in Parchman, Mississippi. Normally the gas would have led to a quick loss of consciousness and death. But eight minutes after his execution began, Gray was seen suffocating and purple-faced, slamming his head against a steel pole.

On May 4, 1990, when the switch was thrown on Joseph Tafero, smoke and six inch flames spewed from his head. The power was stopped and Tafero inhaled deeply several times. Because of the weak electric current, it took two more jolts to kill him.

Such accounts are rare in America. In fact of the 237 executions between 1976 (the year the death penalty was reinstated) and 1994, only 18 have gone awry.[7]

29

"Cruel and unusual" punishment is a rarity in America. This absence of disgraceful deaths makes the vile nature of the cross even more veiled.

The Significance of Disgrace

Because of this veil, we lack a vital piece in our understanding of the death of Jesus. And just as important, we fall short of a full understanding of those texts which raise the cross as the paradigm for Christian living. It is our lack of understanding concerning disgrace which makes the cross an ancient relic or a cheap religious symbol instead of a life-giving paradigm for improving our relationships with others and with God. If we are to fully comprehend the nature of living a cross-centered life, that veil must be lifted. It we want to know the depths of grace, the stench of the cross must be allowed to rise. If we long to understand the demands of discipleship, the shock of crucifixion must be allowed to thrust its way into our hearts. We must rediscover the amazing disgrace of the cross in order to live lives under God's amazing grace.

Perhaps the best way to rediscover the shame of the cross would be to travel back in time to witness a crucifixion first hand. But because of our limitations in time travel, we have to settle for the next best thing. We can listen to the historians of the time as they discuss the cross. We can eavesdrop as they share stories around ancient campfires. Matthew, Mark, Luke, and John opened the door to our understanding of Jesus' crucifixion. But the ancient world had other authors who recorded the disgrace of the cross in a way unmatched by the gospel writers. Crucifixion accounts filled the ancient history books like murder stories fill our newspapers.

In the next chapter, we will sit and listen to these ancient reporters. We'll hear these voices of the past. We'll allow their words to surround us. And we'll begin to rediscover the amazing disgrace of the cross.

Endnotes

1. Josephus, *The Jewish War*, 7.203.

2. John Stott, *The Cross of Christ* (Downers Grove, IL: Inter-Varsity Press, 1986), 23.

3. For a comprehensive treatment of the folly of the "message of the cross" in 1 Corinthians, see Martin Hengel, *Crucifixion in the Ancient World and the Folly of the Message of the Cross* (Philadelphia: Fortress Press, 1977), 1-10.

4. Stott, 21-22; Madeleine Miller, *A Treasury of the Cross* (New York: Harper & Bros, 1956), 21-31.

5. Miller, 184-186.

6. Vassilios Tzaferis, "Jewish Tombs at and Near Giv'at ha-Mivtar, Jerusalem," *Israel Exploration Journal* 20 (1970):18-32; Vassilios Tzaferis, "Crucifixion: The Archaeological Evidence," *Biblical Archaeology Review* 11:1 (January/February 1985):44-53.

7. David Seidman, "A Twist Before Dying," *Time* (May 23, 1994): 52.

Study Questions

1. Read Luke 9:18-22. Why does Jesus equate his identity as the Christ with his mission on the cross?

2. Read Luke 9:23, Galatians 5:24, and Ephesians 5:1-2. What do these verses teach about living *on* the cross when it comes to our relationship with God and with others? (This theme will be covered in detail in later chapters).

3. Read Galatians 2:21; 5:4,11. What do these verses teach about living *under* the cross in our relationship with God and with others? (This theme will also be covered in detail in later chapters).

4. Share a time when you were disgraced.

5. Is it hard for you to picture the cross as disgraceful? Why/Why not?

✝ 2 ✝

A History of Disgrace

Kenneth Bailey tells of visiting the Egyptian village Kom al-Akhdar, where he questioned a man about local traditions. The man began to explain, but others standing near immediately interrupted.

"He wouldn't understand [our traditions] — he is not from this village," they said.

Bailey asked, "How long has he lived here?"

"Only thirty-seven years," they replied.[1]

The villagers assumed that unless you grew up in the presence of the community, you couldn't understand the practices of the community. Unless their ancient stories filled your infant ears, you couldn't grasp their culture. Even thirty-seven years couldn't compensate for a lack of birth experience in the village. A nonnative might be able to quote tradition after tradition. But unless he was truly native, those traditions weren't truly his.

In a sense, the same rule holds for another aspect of ancient culture — crucifixion. Crucifixions were to the ancient culture what sports events are to ours. By the time you could talk and walk, you were exposed to the event. Stories circulated about it. Entire communities witnessed it. But our nonnative standing in that community makes it difficult for us to fully comprehend crucifixion. Our eyes haven't witnessed it. Our ears haven't heard it. Thus we have difficulty seeing what they saw.

Through careful observation, we have gained ground in our comprehension of the cross. Our jewelry imitates its shape. Our music proclaims its results. Our archaeologists unearth its deadly remains. Still, for many, the cross continues to be a concept more academic than emotional. It touches our head but not our heart.

And one element of the cross eludes our investigation — the disgrace of the cross. In the last chapter I suggested that God did not choose the cross simply because of its ability to cause death; God selected it because of its ability to cause disgrace. At its heart, the cross didn't just inflict pain. It also inflicted shame.

That disgrace is what energizes the cross to be a life-changing paradigm for improving our walk with God and with our neighbors. In later chapters we'll see the light the cross sheds on those relationships. In this chapter, however, it is necessary to stop and investigate that disgrace first hand. But our lack of personal experience with the cross makes such investigation a challenge. Are we, like the Egyptian above, destined to be outsiders to the village of the cross and the paradigm it offers for modern life? Fortunately, the answer is no. Stories of crucifixions have been penned by eyewitnesses and preserved by successive generations. While we can't witness those crucifixions first hand, we can read accounts of them. Matthew, Mark, Luke, and John wrote of the most important cross — the cross of Christ. But other ancient authors wrote of other crosses. Their accounts help us better understand that most important cross and its use as a symbol for Christian living.

In this chapter we'll read their true stories. Most of the authors and events will be new to you. The names of the participants may be unfamiliar. But what matters is not the authors or actors. What matters is the story. Their stories are shocking. Some are graphic. But they are necessary if we are to understand the amazing disgrace of the cross.

Age of Disgrace

Before we explore these stories of disgrace, it's important to note the age of disgrace. The cross's garment of disgrace was worn and frayed by the time Jesus wore it. Long before the words of Christ were spoken and the words of the New Testament were written, the disgrace of the cross was commonplace. It wasn't just the government executioners who knew its bitter taste. It wasn't just the historians who understood its shameful stigma. The housewife carrying a jug of water from the well knew. The child writing on a scroll knew. The carpenter picking up wood shavings knew. Their stomachs churned with horror because of the cross. The most common person understood the uncommon disgrace of the cross.

The stench of the cross was known so well because it had lingered for so long. We often credit the Romans with originating crucifixion. But the cross had been tested and retested before the Romans ever laid hands on Jesus.

Ancient history books show that the Persians developed a healthy appetite for the cross long before the Romans. When the Jews returned to Israel from captivity in Babylon, the Persian ruler Cyrus guaranteed their safety during their resettlement. According to an ancient author named Josephus, Cyrus expressed that guarantee in a letter which threatened crucifixion to anyone who hindered the Jews.[2] The Persians also used an early form of crucifixion called impaling. It was cruder than crucifixion in that the victim was simply thrust onto a long sharp stake anchored in the ground. Three ancient historians record a time when the Persian king Darius impaled three thousand men from Babylon.[3]

Other nations besides Persia, however, used crucifixion. Diodorus records at least three other nations familiar with crucifixion. One account tells how Stabrobates, the king of India, threatened his enemies with crucifixion. A second account records the Assyrian king Ninus crucifying the king of a rival nation. A third report shows a queen from Scythia who crucified a rival ruler.[4]

Ancient authors detect the cross's presence in still other cultures. Astyages of the Medes impaled a group of magicians.[5] The Druids often impaled their enemies in pagan temples.[6] The ancient Greeks used crucifixion in their mythical literature as well as in their daily practices.[7]

While many of these cultures contributed to Rome's ultimate use of the cross, it is Carthage which appears to be most directly responsible for the Roman adoption of the practice. Early on, the North African city of Carthage threatened Rome's expansion across the ancient world. In Rome's first war with this potential superpower, the Carthaginians crucified three thousand African soldiers who had deserted to the Romans.[8] Experiences such as this probably led Rome to eventually use crucifixion as a means of disgracing her own enemies.

This brief historical survey shows that crucifixion and the disgrace attached to it were as much a part of the ancient world as football and soccer are to ours. The polluted river of crucifixion wound through pre-Roman history, infecting most major cultures. Only the most remote villages remained untouched by the cross. Thus, while the disgrace of the cross is new to our culture, it was an ugly stain in the very fabric of the ancient culture. The stories from that culture which follow show just how disgraceful the cross truly was.

Anatomy of Disgrace

The disgraceful nature of the cross reveals itself in the events before crucifixion, during crucifixion, and after crucifixion. Each step in the torture was carried out with an eye toward humiliation.

Disgrace before the Cross

Nothing highlights crucifixion's disgrace as much as the precrucifixion rituals. The Gospels alert us to these rituals with their record of the flogging, mocking, and striking of Jesus prior to his own crucifixion (Matt 27:26-31; Mark 15:15-20; John 19:1-16). Other ancient accounts, however, record the precrucifixion ritual in much more detail and of a much worse kind.

For most victims, crucifixion was preceded by flogging or scourging, but other methods were used as well. This torture had only one goal: to demoralize the victim before the main event of the actual crucifixion. One ancient story recounts how Hamilcar, a Carthaginian, plucked his enemy's eyes out and tortured him before his crucifixion.[9] Another account records the Greek myth of Dionysus. According to the myth, Dionysus plucked out the eyes of his enemy, tortured him, and then crucified him.[10] Josephus writes similar graphic stories concerning the Roman crucifixion of Jewish rebels. One account reveals how the Roman commander Florus told his soldiers to scourge and crucify three thousand six hundred Jews living in Jerusalem.[11] Josephus also writes of a young Jew who was stripped and scourged in full view of an entire city in preparation for his threatened crucifixion.[12]

Another ancient author named Philo records one story which shows just how brutal precrucifixion treatment could be. Between 37 to 41 AD, the Egyptian city of Alexandria was governed by a Roman prefect named Flaccus. According to Philo, Flaccus hated the local Jews so intensely that he conducted ethnic cleansing. Jews were stabbed and dragged through the streets. Stones and clubs bruised their bodies. Fire torched their skin. Other Jews were tied to the ground for Flaccus's men to jump up and down on them. Those who died were dragged through the streets again until their skin and muscles fell off.

Survivors were forced to endure even more. They and their relatives were treated to what Philo describes in these words: "[They] were arrested, scourged, tortured, and after all these outrages, which were all their bodies could make room for, the final punishment kept in reserve for them was the cross."[13] Flaccus tried to "fill up the body" with as much pain as possible before crucifixion. Yet Philo implies that the cross was still more painful and shameful than even the worst precrucifixion treatment.

Had death been the only objective, these victims would have been taken straight to the cross. Since disgrace was also an objective, slow torture was given before the cross. That torture often took place in public. Had pain been the only objective, the precrucifixion treatment would have occurred behind closed doors with only the victim and the executioner present. Since disgrace was also an objective, the public was invited.

The public nature of the precrucifixion treatment is highlighted by the fact that ancient authors often describe it as a spectacle. Executioners turned what might have been a painful but personal experience into grisly public entertainment. As we continue to explore Philo's account of Alexandria, we find evidence of this. Flaccus, the Roman prefect, ordered those who survived the precrucifixion treatment to be hung on some sort of wheel, brutally mauled, and paraded through the middle of a stadium to their crosses. The condemned were followed by dancers, mimes, and flute players.[14] A festival air filled these crucifixions. The parade of the condemned satisfied the public's hunger for entertainment.

The Cross: Saved by the Shame of It All

Disgrace on the Cross

The paint of disgrace applied so liberally before the crucifixion continued to be brushed on during the crucifixion. Jesus' own crucifixion took place in the midst of a mob. Crowds of people gathered as Jesus and the two criminals were erected on their timbers (Matt 27:32-56; Mark 15:21-41; Luke 23:26-49; John 19:17-30). Jesus' crucifixion was a public display intended to degrade him.

Other nonbiblical writers record the same public nature of the actual crucifixion itself. In 73 BC, a large slave revolt broke out in the gladiator's barracks near Naples, Italy. A man named Spartacus led the revolt which lasted two years. At the end of the uprising, six thousand slaves who had been captured were crucified. Their crucifixions didn't take place in the private setting of a prison courtyard. Their crosses were set up along the Appian Way, a major road in the Roman transportation system.[15] It would be comparable to crucifying six thousand people along a modern interstate.

Josephus also records the public and degrading nature of the crucifixion itself. After Alexander Jannaeus crucified eight hundred Jewish men during his dinner, he had their wives and children slaughtered in front of the dying men.[16]

Even worse are the antics of Antiochus Epiphanes who invaded Judea in 169 BC. Epiphanes punished the Jewish families who disobeyed his command to stop circumcising their children. He whipped and mutilated the fathers. Then he nailed them to crosses. Their wives and sons were then strangled in front of the still breath-

40

ing men. Finally, the children were hung from the necks of their crucified parents.[17]

Josephus reports an account involving the Roman commander Titus, who was sent by Rome to extinguish a Jewish uprising in Israel. Titus and his armies inflicted numerous losses on the Jewish rebels. When the heat of the battle began to die, Titus's soldiers killed time by nailing the bodies of their Jewish prisoners in different postures on the walls of Jerusalem.[18] These acts were done solely to degrade the victims. The soldiers didn't just want to cause pain. They didn't just want to bring death. They also longed to bring disgrace. The actual event of the crucifixion served a shame-full purpose.

Disgrace after the Cross

Even the events after death illustrate the disgrace of the cross. Ancient historians reveal that at times, bodies of those killed by other means were then crucified in an attempt to bring shame on the dead and those associated with them. Three stories tell of three notable figures in antiquity who suffered the degradation of crucifixion after death. One figure named Cyrus was killed and his hands and head were cut off. Handless and headless, his body was then impaled on a stake.[19] Another named Achaeus also had his extremities cut off after being killed. His body was then crucified. He suffered the further humiliation of having his head sown up in the skin of a donkey, an animal of ridicule in the ancient world.[20] Finally, a figure named Albinus was attacked and killed by his enemy Severus. Severus cut off Albinus' head and had it sent to Rome

41

to be publicly displayed on a pole "so that the Roman people could see for themselves the measure of his temper . . . ."[21]

Crucifixion thus humiliated even the dead. Although the body no longer breathed, it could still be subject to disgrace by being hung publicly on a stake or a cross.

Perhaps the best ancient story highlighting the disgrace of the cross is no story at all. It is a painting — actually, a piece of ancient graffiti. Sometime during the third century AD, an anonymous artist scarred the Roman Palestine with a crude drawing. The drawing shows a crucified man. The body of the man is normal, but his head is that of a donkey — an animal of disgrace. Below the crucified figure is another man, apparently expressing adoration to the victim. One line of text below the drawing says this: "Alexamenos worships [his] god."[22] The drawing probably represented the feelings of many Romans toward Christianity. Christians should have been ashamed to worship someone who had been crucified. They may as well have worshiped a donkey.

Analysis of Disgrace

This gruesome tour through ancient literature shows that crucifixion captured the worst of imaginations and pushed the human body to the limit. The cross served effectively as a method of death. Few survived the combination of torture before and during crucifixion. Of all ancient accounts there is perhaps only one instance of someone surviving a crucifixion. Josephus records finding three of his acquaintances among others who had been crucified in a town called Tekoa. The three, still living, were immediately removed from their crosses. Only one survived.[23] This survivor is likely the lone exception in the annals of crucifixion literature. Each victim dreaded the cross because of its power to kill. As Philo recorded earlier, crucifixion was the final punishment when the body had all it could hold. The cross served effectively as a method of death.

But more importantly, the cross served effectively as a method of disgrace. With the cross, the full force of the executioner's hatred could be unleashed in full view of onlookers. Even after death, the presence of the body or head on the cross served as a dark reminder of the recent disgrace. This disgrace was known by the commoner and the king. Martin Hengel, one of the foremost experts on crucifixion, summarizes it in this way: ". . . it was a matter of subjecting the victim to the utmost indignity."[24]

As the early Christians read biblical texts which used the cross as a paradigm for living, this disgraceful nature of the cross rose in their hearts and minds. In the next section, we'll begin to look at those texts.

Endnotes

1. Kenneth E. Bailey, "Informal Controlled Oral Tradition and the Synoptic Gospels," *Themelios* 20:2 (January 1995): 6.

2. Josephus, *Jewish Antiquities*, 11.17.

3. Herodotus, *Herodotus*, 3.159, 3.132; Thucydides, *Thucydides*, 1.110.3; Xenophon, *Anabasis*, 3.1.7.

4. Diodorus, *Diodorus of Sicily*, 2.18.1-2; 2.1.10; 2.44.2.

5. Herodotus, 1.127-128.

6. Strabo, *The Geography of Strabo*, 4.4.5.

7. Diodorus, 18.16.1-3; Polybius, *The Histories*, 8.21.1-3; Diodorus, 3.65.5-6; Lucian, *On Sacrifices*, 6.

8. Appian, *Of Sicily and the Other Islands*, 5.3.

9. Diodorus, 25.10.1-2.

10. Ibid., 3.65.5-6.

11. Josephus, *The Jewish War*, 2.306-307.

12. Ibid., 7.200

13. Philo, *In Flaccum*, 72.

14. Ibid., 85.

15. Jo Ann Shelton, *As The Romans Did* (New York: Oxford University Press, 1988), 182.

16. Josephus, *Jewish Antiquities*, 13.380.

17. Ibid., 12.256.

18. Josephus, *The Jewish War*, 5.451.

19. Xenophon, 3.1.7.

20. Polybius, 8.21.1-3.

21. Herodian, *Herodian*, 3.8.1.

22. "A Crucified Donkey," in *New Documents Illustrating Early Christianity. A Review of the Greek Inscriptions and Papyri Published in 1979*, vol. 4, ed. G.R. Horsley (North Ryde, New South Wales: The Ancient History Documentary Research Centre, Macquarie University, 1987), 137 no. 34, citing G.M.A. Hanfman in *A Tribute to P.H. Von Blanckenhagen*, ed. G. Kopcke and M.B. Moore (Locust Valley, 1979), 205-207.

23. Josephus, *The Life*, 420-421.

24. Martin Hengel, *Crucifixion in the Ancient World and the Folly of the Message of the Cross* (Philadelphia: Fortress Press, 1977), 24.

Study Questions

1. What are some events in our modern society which are as much a part of our culture as crucifixion was to the ancient culture?

2. Explain why so much torture and abuse was conducted before crucifixion when the crucifixion itself was sufficient to kill its victim.

3. How would it feel to be walking along the Appian Way and see 6,000 crucified slaves along its path?

4. What is the significance of the crucified donkey?

Part Two

Part Two

Living under the Cross
A Life of Celebration

It's one thing to understand the cross's disgrace. It's another to understand the implications that disgrace has for living in relationship with God and with others. The one who died on the cross of crosses and those who followed him used the cross as the symbol for kingdom living. It exemplified the generous nature of grace. It illustrated the demanding nature of discipleship. It showed how to live with God. It portrayed how to live with others.

In one sense, we are called to live *under* the cross in a life of celebration. Under the cross, we celebrate freedom from the deadly consequences of our failures. We dance with joy in the light of the grace-filled fires of the cross.

In another sense, we are called to live *on* the cross in a life of service. On the cross, we serve in imitation of the one who first hung there. We die daily on the rough-hewn timbers of the cross.

The Cross: Saved by the Shame of It All

The disgrace of the cross illuminates what it means to live *under* and *on* the cross. In the next two chapters, we'll explore the breathtaking celebration that can take place under the cross. We'll see just how amazing God's disgrace can be. And we'll explore how that life under the cross affects our walk with God and with neighbor.

✝ 3 ✝

When Demons Danced

The Tyranny of Failure and Forgiveness

Peter Andrews writes for *Golf Digest* magazine. Recently, he wrote about the tyranny of the handicap — that critical number assigned to a golfer based on his or her ability. Listen to Andrews's lament:

> Convicts in a penitentiary have a better time of it than many golfers. Apart from the stigma of wearing a number in the first place, no moral judgement is attached to a prisoner's numeral. . . . It is different with the golfer. A golfer's handicap, like Marley's length of chain, has been forged link by link and must be carried wherever he goes. . . . I am an 18-handicapper and hate being so. It is not fair. . . . I drive farther than an 18. I putt better than an 18. . . . Therein lies the tragedy of golf. We know what should be, but there is always some number telling us what is. . . . One of the dreariest bromides of golf says there is no room for descriptive passages on a scorecard. There should be. Scorecards

51

ought to be expanded so there is space for a brief essay.
. . . When you have cobbled together a 7 on [a par 4]
hole, an explanation is called for. . . .[1]

Andrew's essay, meant as a description of the life of a
golfer, aptly describes the life of a Christian. We know
what we should be, but there is always some mistake
telling us what is. We feel like saints, but our failures
remind us we are sinners. At times we know that we are
more holy than an 18. But another mistake justifies the
handicap. At times we know that we are more godly
than an 18. But frequent failures slap us with reality.
We know what we should be. We know what we are in
rare moments. But there is always some sin telling us
what really is.

And as much as we'd like a chance to explain, there
isn't space. "Yes God, I goofed up, but . . . ." Like golf
there is no room. No essays. No explanation. No elabo-
ration. Just the truth. As a result, there is little freedom
in our faith. There is little "wow" in our worship. We
want to be warmed by the fires of celebration. We want
to dance with joy. But failures douse the flames of celebration. Mistakes trip our steps of joy. What should be
a life of triumph is one of tragedy. What should be ter-
rific is simply tyranny.

But as the music of joy fades, the tune of words from
Colossians fills our ears: "When you were dead in your
sins and in the uncircumcision of your sinful nature,
God made you alive with Christ. He forgave us all our
sins" (Col 2:13).

Paul sings about our past. The first stanza sounds of
living and dying. Spiritually, our casket was sealed and

the grave was dug. We were dead. The second stanza portrays ancient Jewish rituals. Spiritually, our bodies were covered with filthy flesh begging to be removed. We were uncircumcised. Both verses portray the reality of our failures. Both describe what truly was. Both show our handicap.

But Paul's song doesn't stop. He sings two more stanzas — not of our past, but of our present. The first line tells of living and dying. We have been made alive together with Christ. Spiritually, the casket is open and our bodies course with life. The second line tells of gift giving. We have received the gift of forgiveness. Spiritually, every mistake is erased.

These words are intended to resurrect celebration. But their familiarity often leaves celebration flat on its back. Our eyes have tracked these words before. Our hands have touched them repeatedly. Our ears treat them like the jingle of an outdated commercial. This is the same old message about the same old rugged cross. And the routine nature of Paul's song may leave us with questions:

"If God made us alive and forgiven, why do I still feel dead and condemned?"

"Why does my handicap still feel so real."

"Why can't I shake my past?"

You may understand Paul's words. But you may not experience his words. They may make sense on paper. But they lose credibility in the ebb and flow of daily living.

Perhaps knowing the tyranny of the familiar, Paul continues. He develops his theme in a way that moves the hardest of hearts. Paul moves beyond dry theological concepts about grace, and illustrates them with something hard and gritty — something that cannot be ignored. Paul points to the cross and its disgrace to convince his readers and us of the undeniable reality of a grace beyond belief.

Overdue IOUs

Paul punctures our hardened hearts with another verse. It is a verse of debt and payment:

> . . . having canceled the written code, with its regulations, that was against us and that stood opposed to us; he took it away, nailing it to the cross (Col 2:14).

The centerpiece of this song is the word "written code". The word doesn't refer to the Old Testament. Paul isn't saying that God's grace is illustrated by the nailing of the Old Testament to the cross. Neither does "written code" refer to specific parts of the Old Testament like the Law of Moses or the Ten Commandments. Paul isn't saying that grace is found in the fact that Christ killed these on his cross.

In Paul's day, the word "written code" referred to a special kind of document. The word literally means "hand written". It refers to a note of indebtedness written in one's own hand as proof of an obligation. Usually the note contained penalty clauses. The author of the note was to pay back certain dues under threat of penalty.[2]

Today we call such notes IOUs. The letter of Philemon is an example of one such "written code." In it, Paul states that his handwritten document is proof of his obligation to pay back outstanding dues:

If he has done you any wrong or owes you anything, charge it to me. I, Paul, am writing this with my own hand. I will pay it back (Phlm 18-19).

When I was a graduate student in Memphis, Tennessee, I worked part time as an intern at a campus ministry next to the University of Memphis. Each Thursday afternoon brought hundreds of hungry students to our $2.00 lunches. Inevitably, some students forgot wallets or purses, so they received an IOU which they were required to sign. The students were then under obligation to pay that due.

In a similar way, Paul implies that we are under obligation to pay a spiritual due. God summoned us to a standard that we haven't met. Our refusal to play par led to a penalty. That penalty is described earlier by Paul's words "dead" and "uncircumcised." Absent-minded students in Memphis fought with IOUs requiring $2.00 for lunch. All of us fight with IOUs requiring death for our failures committed over the course of life. We cannot rip up, burn, or destroy these IOUs. They cannot be erased or eliminated.

But according to Paul, Jesus did three things to our IOU at the cross. First, Jesus "canceled" it. Literally, Paul writes that Jesus "wiped it away." Jesus took that deadly IOU and erased your name from it. He blotted it out. He wiped the writing off.[3]

Second, Jesus "took the IOU away." He grabbed it from our hands. He lifted it from our pockets. He ran as far away with it as he could.

Third, Jesus "nailed it to the cross." Jesus drove a spike through its heart, forever fixing it to his timbers.

This third point may be an allusion to the Roman practice of nailing a criminal's charge to the top of his cross.[4] Jesus took *our* charge and nailed it to the top of *his* cross.

Colossians 2:15 shows how all of this took place. Here Paul allows the disgrace of the cross to ooze across his page. But this disgrace finds an unlikely victim: "And having disarmed the powers and authorities, he made a public spectacle of them, triumphing over them by the cross."

Spiritual powers and authorities, not human powers and authorities, were the real victims of the cross. That fact makes little sense apart from the material covered in the last chapter. The disgrace-filled stories from the ancient world are vital to understanding the blow this verse deals. The disgrace of the cross allowed our IOU to be fully paid.

Disarming Demons

Three words are crucial in this verse. The first word is "disarm." The word has a dual meaning. In one sense it means to strip or to take off someone's clothes. Just as Jesus was physically stripped for his crucifixion, the satanic powers and authorities were spiritually stripped. Stripping a person signified humiliation. Without clothes, we become vulnerable and defenseless. Naked we are disgraced. Paul says it wasn't Jesus who was disgraced on the cross. It was the satanic powers. Jesus spiritually stripped them. He made them stark naked.

The word "disarm" also means to weaken.[5] When you strip a person, you weaken them. They become unable

to exert their strength. By describing Jesus as the dis-
armer of demons, Paul is referring to a specific kind of
disarming. The cross didn't weaken demons physically.
It weakened them spiritually.

The only strength satanic powers and authorities have
is their power of accusation. They can go chin to chin
with God and accuse us. They can point to our IOUs and
demand payment. Their power is the power I had as an
intern at the campus ministry in Memphis. Once or twice
a semester we demanded payment of all IOUs. Until the
IOU was paid, we possessed great power over the delin-
quent students. If we wanted, we could threaten double
payment next time. If we desired, we could revoke special
privileges until payment arrived. If we thought it necessary, we could assign after-lunch cleaning duties to the
student whose IOU we held. Unpaid IOUs gave us power.
But when payment arrived, either by the student or a
friend of the student, power turned to putty.

Unpaid spiritual IOUs mean power for demons. But
when payment arrived, their power turned to putty.
Jesus disarmed spiritual forces of evil by removing their
only power — the power of accusation. Since Jesus paid
our IOU, there can be no more accusations. Every time
we fail, God tells the accusing demonic powers that our
debt has been paid. Regardless of the seriousness of our
sins or the frequency of our failures, our IOU stands
nailed to the cross of Christ. "Paid-In-Full" is all God
sees. Thus these evil spiritual forces may as well be
naked. They have no power anymore.

Yet while Paul paints these accusing demons as
naked and powerless, we often treat them as clothed

and powerful. We often replay the mistakes and failures of others, refusing to forgive them for what has passed. We cannot get over that husband's insensitive remark last week. We cannot overlook that coworker's ineptness last month. We cannot move beyond the caustic statements made by a friend in a heated discussion.

Or just as bad, we resurrect our own sins and beat ourselves over the head with them. Yesterday's lie, last month's lust, and last year's laziness become whips with which we inflict penance on ourselves. Yet that replay denies the truth of the cross. When we accuse ourselves or others for past mistakes, we engage in activity that Satan himself can no longer practice. Even Satan cannot accuse us for our sins. That power has been stripped from him. Thus how can we accuse ourselves? How can we live in the past of mistakes? Paul's words bring freedom from the past. It is not we who are disgraced. It is not Jesus who was disgraced. It is the demonic powers and authorities. As a result, we can stand free of the past.

Indecent Exposure

A second crucial word in Colossians 2:15 is the phrase "made a public spectacle of them." Literally Paul writes that Jesus "exposed them in public." Like the previous word, this is a phrase of disgrace. Its shamefull tone is illustrated in Matthew 1:18-19:

> This is how the birth of Jesus Christ came about: His mother Mary was pledged to be married to Joseph, but before they came together, she was found to be with child through the Holy Spirit. Because Joseph her husband was a righteous man and did not want to *expose*

her to public disgrace, he had in mind to divorce her quietly (emphasis mine).

The word "expose" is the same word translated "make a public spectacle" found in Colossians 2:15. Joseph didn't want Mary's condition to become tabloid headlines. He didn't want to expose her to the public.

Jesus, however, did want those things for the satanic powers and authorities. He wanted them to head the tabloids. He wanted to subject them to public humiliation. While Jesus was physically ridiculed on the cross, the powers of Satan were spiritually ridiculed. Jesus exposed them in public. Their nakedness was not a private thing. Jesus invited a crowd to witness their shame. All of heaven looked on as these powers were humiliated and disgraced.

I Love a Parade

The final, and perhaps most important word in this text is the word "triumphing." This word refers to a triumphal procession. It should remind us of the images from Philo's story of the procession of near-dead Jews in Alexandria. Just as those Jews were paraded through a crowded stadium with flute players and mimes following them, these evil powers were paraded before all of heaven and marched to their own crosses. In other ancient literature, this word referred to the action a king would take with the head of his decapitated enemy. He would display it publicly on a pole to show his victory.[6]

Spiritually, Jesus did just that to these spiritual powers of evil. Those who would accuse us before God because of our sins have been totally disgraced. They stand naked, in public, and have been paraded to their own death. All because of the cross of Christ.

What Paul describes is a great reversal. As these satanic powers conducted the crucifixion of Jesus, they found themselves subject to their own crucifixion. As they stripped Jesus of his clothes, their own clothes dropped. As they gathered a crowd to mock Jesus, a crowd gathered to mock them. And as they paraded Jesus shamefully before others, they themselves were led in shameful procession. Each nail they placed in the body of Jesus found its way to their own bodies. The result was the demolition of every IOU, and thus the demolition of the power of accusation.

Recently, the necessity of the cross has been questioned. Some of those doubts were caught in the April 4, 1994 edition of *Christianity Today*. Delores Williams, a feminist theologian, said this about the cross: "I don't think we need folks hanging on crosses and blood dripping and weird stuff." Another theologian exclaimed, "If we cannot imagine Jesus as a tree, as a river, as wind, and as rain, we are doomed together."[7]

Paul takes the opposite stand. If we cannot imagine Jesus as a crucified and disgraced man, we are doomed together. Without his disgrace, our spiritual enemies would never be disgraced. We need folks hanging on crosses. We need blood dripping. Without that, we are doomed together. But because of that, we can dance together. Our debt has been paid. Our penalty has been removed. We thus no longer have to live in the past of our failures or the failures of others. Every sin has met its match. All because of the amazing disgrace of the cross.

Endnotes

1. Peter Andrews, "The Tyranny and Tragedy of Numbers," *Golf Digest* 46:2 (February 1995): 146-147.

2. "χειρόγραφον," Walter Bauer, *A Greek-English Lexicon of the New Testament and Other Early Christian Literature*, translated by William F. Arndt and F. Wilbur Gingrich (Chicago: University of Chicago Press, 1979), 880; also Peter T. O'Brien, *Word Biblical Commentary: Colossians, Philemon* (Dallas: Word Books, 1982), 124-125.

3. "ἐξαλείφω," Bauer, 272.

4. "προσηλόω," Bauer, 714.

5. "ἀπεκδύομαι," Bauer, 83; O'Brien, *Word*, 126.

6. "θριαμβεύω," Bauer, 363.

7. Susan Cyre, "Fallout Escalates Over 'Goddess' Sophia Worship," *Christianity Today* (April 4, 1994): 74.

Study Questions

1. Have there been times when you felt you had a spiritual handicap? Explain.

2. How has that handicap doused the flames of celebration God wants you to experience?

3. Is there someone in your life whose mistakes you constantly replay for them? What do you need to do to overcome your fixation on what has already passed?

4. What sin in your own life have you allowed to dictate your present? Read Colossians 2:13-15 and pray that you would better understand the reality of those verses in your life.

5. How does this description of the cross impact your relationship with God?

✕ 4 ✕

Scorecard Christianity
Part 1

The 200 Club. Not a cable talk show for Christians. Not an award for real estate agents. But an elite organization among members of my high school football team. Our coaches developed the club to motivate us to do more weight lifting. Officially, members of the 200 Club received a free t-shirt. Unofficially, they received playing privileges on the field.

Everyone on the team wanted in. And there was only one entrance requirement: you had to bench press 200 pounds. Few in our 1A school could accomplish such a feat. As a result, the club was small and exclusive.

You may not have had a 200 Club growing up, but you can probably relate to it. Our lives are filled with "clubs," both formal and informal, which require certain scores to get in.

To get in (and stay in) most graduate schools, students must have a 3.0 GPA. Once the GPA drops, the student is placed on provisional status. If the low GPA persists, the student is expelled and can only be re-admitted after five years.

To get in many health insurance programs, applicants must score well on a physical exam and on questions related to a variety of health issues.

Often, another "club" is viewed similarly: the club of heaven. Just as many earthly clubs award membership only to those who earn a high enough score, many today believe that heaven awards membership only to those who earn a high enough score. The 1990 film "Ghost," starring Patrick Swayze, Demi Moore, and Whoopi Goldberg illustrates this scorecard view of Christianity. The film won two Oscars — one for best original screenplay, and one for best supporting actress. But it bombed when it came to correct theology.

The film told the story of a successful businessman who was irreligious and lived with a woman to whom he wasn't married. Nonetheless, he was a decent sort of man. After dying in a mugging, he chose to remain on earth as a ghost so he could protect Demi Moore from the same hoodlums who had killed him. Throughout the film, people's eternal resting places were determined not by any religious criteria, but solely by their deeds. Those who pursued the demise of others entered darkness. Those who served others entered light. Heaven was for those who earned a high enough score.

This scorekeeping philosophy is also reflected in a 1994 study conducted by the Barna Research Group. In the study, 54% of those asked said they believed that if people are good enough, they will earn a place in heaven, regardless of their religious beliefs.[1] According to Barna, over half of us hold to scorecard Christianity — a belief that in order to get in heaven, you must earn a high enough score.

"Ghost" and Barna show that, for some, religion plays no part in that score. But even those of us who believe religion has something to do with getting to heaven can easily fall into scorecard thinking. While I worked as an intern at the Highland Street Church of Christ in Memphis, the ministry staff met once a week. During one meeting the topic turned to salvation and heaven. Jim, our song leader, voiced the words we all thought but wouldn't admit: "I feel guilty being saved by grace. I should be saved by works."

Intuitively, scorecard religion sounds right. It's the way it ought to be. It is easier to trust in "I Want to Be a Worker" than in "Amazing Grace."

This struggle with scorecard thinking is not new. In fact, since Christianity's beginning, the Christian message and scorecard philosophies have been married in a perverted relationship. The letter of Galatians is *the* address to this philosophy.

Jumping for Justification

Galatians 2:15-16 summarizes the entire letter:

We who are Jews by birth and not "Gentile sinners" know that a man is not justified by observing the law, but by faith in Jesus Christ. So we, too, have put our faith in Christ Jesus that we may be justified by faith in Christ and not by observing the law, because by observing the law no one will be justified.

The word "justified" stands at the center of this text.

It is a fancy word for a simple concept — being heaven bound. It means to be in the clear, to be right with God, to be pronounced righteous.[2] It is the green light into the gates of heaven.

According to Paul, there are two ways to be justified. The wrong way is by observing what he calls "the law," or more literally, "works of the law."

Those few words illuminate the situation which prompted Paul's letter. These innocent Christians in Galatia were infiltrated by some not-so-innocent preachers. As the preachers pulled into town, they set up shop on the curb and sold their snake oil of false teaching. Based on the reference to "law" in Galatians, these preachers must have advocated a number of things from the Old Testament for these New Testament Christians to do. They didn't think that believing in Jesus was enough to ensure heaven. Thus they presented a list of extra things someone had to do to get into heaven. These extra requirements included things like circumcision, eating the right foods, observing holy days, and being associated with the right kind of people.

Paul had no quarrel with some of these things by themselves. If someone wanted to be circumcised or eat certain foods, that was his choice. But Paul did have a problem with the implication that these actions added to one's spiritual score. Paul's comments above show this was never God's intent.

The traveling preachers used an argument like this: "If you want to be a real Jew (which, by the way, is the only way to get to heaven), here is the score you must earn and the items you must complete to earn that score. . . ." With sarcasm lacing his words, Paul writes that even a real Jew, one from birth (who, by the way, is the only one going to heaven), knows that no one can get to heaven based on a score. Thus Paul denies any validity to the scorecard view.

Paul is not waging war here against the Old Testament. Paul doesn't take issue with these Christians because they relish certain Old Testament relics. Paul takes issue with them because they advocate scorecard religion. They believe that in order to get right with God, you have to get working on your score.

Neither is Paul waging war against the idea that you must do certain things to get to heaven. Even Paul taught that some things were necessary in order to be right with God. What Paul battles here is the idea that by doing these things, you earn a certain score. And only a high enough score guarantees passage to Paradise.

This scorekeeping tendency didn't just annoy Paul. It infuriated him. Several places throughout the letter, his emotions betray how deeply he dislikes scorekeeping. Anger spills over in the beginning of the letter. Normally, Paul followed the customary form of letter writing by including a word of thanks at the beginning of his letters. Galatians, however, contains no such thanksgiving. Paul is so upset that normal etiquette doesn't have a chance. Instead, he begins his letter in this way:

> I am astonished that you are so quickly deserting the one who called you . . . . But even if we or an angel from heaven should preach a gospel other than the one we preached to you, let him be eternally condemned! As we have already said, so now I say again: If anybody is

preaching to you a gospel other than what you accepted, let him be eternally condemned (1:6,8-9)!

Anger rises again in 3:1,3: "You foolish Galatians! Who has bewitched you? . . . Are you so foolish?"

Rage overflows in 5:12: "As for those agitators, I wish they would go the whole way and emasculate themselves!" To those saying that circumcision earned a high score, Paul wished the knife would slip as they performed the ceremony on themselves. Paul wished physical harm on scorekeepers.

Thus Paul doesn't just shake his head at this philosophy. He shakes his fist. He doesn't just speculate. He screams. He doesn't just talk. He threatens. We might think that scorecard Christianity is no big deal. For Paul, however, it was the biggest deal. Paul gets angrier at Christians living a good life who think that life will get them into heaven, than he does at Christians living a bad life who think that life will keep them from heaven.

And the reason for Paul's anger is found only at the cross. The cross is the spring from which Paul's emotions flow. Only in the shameful light of the cross are the flaws of scorecard religion revealed. Using the cross and its well-known disgrace, Paul makes five deadly points against scorecard religion.

Flaw #1: It's Not The Real Thing

First, Paul states that scorecard Christianity isn't even Christianity:

I am astonished that you are so quickly deserting the one who called you by the grace of Christ and are turning to a different gospel — which is really no gospel at

all. Evidently some people are throwing you into confusion and are trying to pervert the gospel of Christ (1:6-7).

Paul accuses these Christians of desertion. The word
"deserting" means to move from one school of thought
to another, or to change geographical locations.[3] Those
who believed in scorecards were on the move. Where
they moved from is indicated by the words "the one who
called you." When we buy into scorecard Christianity,
we have deserted God himself. God has so little to do
with scorecards that those who hold them will have
little to do with God.

Paul also charges these Christians with turning to a
different gospel. Literally, Paul writes that they are
turning to "another" gospel which is not "another" gospel.
The two words translated "another" are actually two different words. One word means another of a similar
kind. The other word means another of a completely different kind.[4] The first word might be used for different
kinds of apples. If I just finished a Washington apple,
and asked for "another" (the first word), you might give
me a Granny Smith apple. While the Granny Smith
apple is different from my Washington apple, it is still
an apple. But if you gave me an orange, the second
"another" would describe the orange. Or if you gave me
a brick, the second word would apply. Paul says those
who preach a scorecard gospel aren't just opting for a
different gospel of a similar kind. They are buying into
something that doesn't even resemble the gospel. They
are taking oranges and bricks for apples.

Paul's words in 2:19-20 also illustrate how far removed
scorecard Christianity is from real Christianity:

The Cross: Saved by the Shame of It All

> For through the law I died to the law so that I might live for God. I have been crucified with Christ and I no longer live, but Christ lives in me. The life I live in the body, I live by faith in the Son of God, who loved me and gave himself for me.

Paul says that he has been spiritually crucified to the law, or scorecard Christianity. When someone was crucified to something, they were radically separated from that thing. Those crucified to physical life were permanently separated from physical life. Josephus's lone account of a crucifixion survivor shows just how effectively crucifixion separated people from something. They were shamed and disgraced to the point of no return. Paul says a similar event occurred between him and scorekeeping. He was crucified to a life of keeping score. These Christians, however, were attempting to reverse that crucifixion. Returning to scorekeeping would be as unnatural as a crucifixion victim returning from shameful death to physical life.

Paul repeats these thoughts in 5:4: "You who are trying to be justified by law have been alienated from Christ; you have fallen from grace." In Rom 7:2, the word "alienated" is used of a wife whose husband has died. The two are alienated from one another. They no longer have association with one another. Here, Paul writes that when Christians resort to scorecards, Jesus becomes a stranger. We no longer have association with him. We literally fall from grace.

Thus Paul says that scorecard Christianity has nothing to do with real Christianity. Assuming that scores come with Christianity is like assuming that a college degree comes with free dinners at Red Lobster. It's like assuming that buying a home comes with a trip on the space shuttle. The two have absolutely nothing to do with each other. If you find yourself keeping score and hoping yours is high enough to get into heaven, Paul implies you have never experienced real Christianity. Christianity has nothing to do with scorekeeping.

Flaw #2: It Cancels the Cross

Second, Paul states that scorecard Christianity voids the cross. In 5:2, Paul writes about the effect of such beliefs on the cross: "Mark my words! I, Paul, tell you that if you let yourselves be circumcised, Christ will be of no value to you at all."

Paul warns that if these Christians give in to just one scorekeeping idea like circumcision, they would make Christ useless. Scorecard religion makes the life and death of Jesus as necessary as a sandbox in the desert, a saltshaker in the ocean, or a fireplace in the summer.

Paul makes a similar statement in 2:21: "I do not set aside the grace of God, for if righteousness could be gained through the law, Christ died for nothing!" Here, Paul states the hypothetical. If scorecard religion was right, Jesus died for nothing. If God kept score and granted entrance to only certain scores, the cross happened for no reason.

Recently, several friends and I helped construct two church buildings in Chihuahua City, Mexico. The road to the work site took us through a major intersection of the city each day. When the stoplight turned red, teenagers would rush our van with squeegee and sprayer expecting money for washing the windshield. We usually encountered these teenage entrepreneurs at the end of the day when we were tired of working and giving. Thus when they rushed the van, one of our drivers would yell "gratis" meaning "free." He wanted them to know that if they washed the windshield, it would be for free. It would be for no reason.

That's what Paul is saying about the cross and scores. If scorecard religion is valid, Jesus' death is invalid. It is for no reason. It is "gratis."

Most of the crucifixion stories we examined in earlier chapters showed someone crucified for a reason. Jewish rebels died for their freedom. Kings died for their nations. But imagine being crucified for no reason. Imagine the mocking and torture of the precrucifixion treatment. Imagine the death parade through crowds of people to the crucifixion site. Imagine hanging above the ground naked, on display for the entire city. Imagine slow and painful death. Then imagine it was for no reason. Imagine a mistake was made. There was no need for the crucifixion. There was no benefit to the sacrifice.

Some useless actions can be mistaken for significant actions without great cost to the one performing them. For my first two years at New Mexico State University, each day I would leave class and go immediately to my dorm room to memorize the day's notes. One day, my wife Kendra and another friend pointed out there was no need for such a sacrifice. I could accomplish the same thing by studying the notes the week before the test. For two years I performed an action which was unnecessary. But I didn't lose a great deal by doing it —

except some extra play time. Perhaps you've made the bed one morning and your spouse tells you, "You didn't need to do that; I'm going to wash those sheets today." Maybe you've filled out paperwork for a job interview only to find out later that you didn't need to fill out that particular paper. Actions like these are annoying and inconvenient, but nothing's really lost in doing them.

Crucifixion on the other hand was far more than annoying and inconvenient. It was the most disgrace-filled and death-filled event one could endure. It was literally a once in a lifetime experience. Paul says that if scorecard religion is what Christianity is all about, Jesus' cross was for nothing. It was all a mistake.

"We're sorry sir, but you didn't need to do that. If you'll come down off the cross, we'll see if we can work out this mistake. We are really sorry for the mix up." Such an apology hardly seems appropriate in the face of the cross. Yet if scorecard religion is true, that's all Jesus gets for his effort. There is no amazing disgrace. There is just wasted disgrace.

In the rest of his letter, Paul explains why these first two points are true. Remaining at the cross, Paul shows why scorecards have nothing to do with real Christianity, and why scorecards invalidate what happened at the cross. In the next chapter, we'll explore these final three flaws to scorecard Christianity.

Endnotes

1. Barna Research Group, "Currents," *Discipleship Journal* 86 (March/April 1995): 14.

2. "δικαιόω," Walter Bauer, *A Greek-English Lexicon of the New*

Testament and Other Early Christian Literature, translated by William F. Arndt and F. Wilbur Gingrich (Chicago: University of Chicago Press, 1979), 197.

3. "μετατίθημι," Bauer, 513; Richard N. Longenecker, *Word Biblical Commentary: Galatians* (Dallas: Word Books, 1990), 14-15.

4. "ἕτερος," Bauer, 315; "ἄλλος," Bauer, 39-40.

Study Questions

1. The movie "Ghost," the research by Barna, and the comment by a minister illustrate the prevalence of scorecard thinking. What are some other modern examples of this type of thinking in our society?

2. Why do you think the scorecard philosophy is such a popular way of thinking about our relationship to God?

3. This chapter focuses mostly on keeping score in our relationship with God, but what does scorecard thinking do to our relationships in marriage, at work, in the neighborhood, and with the lost?

4. The scores which the preachers in Galatia advocated were earned by things like circumcision and the observance of certain days. What are modern examples of things which many of us believe earn high scores with God?

5. Has scorecard thinking been a part of your walk with God? How does it affect your day-to-day relationship with him? In what ways does your evaluation of your relationship with God depend on your recent "scores" in key areas of your life?

6. A friend just read this chapter and said to you, "Since God doesn't require scores, I guess it really doesn't matter how I live my life." What would you say to him/her? What purpose does a holy life and the compassionate treatment of others have if it doesn't earn our spot in heaven?

✝ **5** ✝

Scorecard Christianity
Part 2

According to William Bennett, in his best selling book *The Book of Virtues*, a poem by Marian Douglas was among the first reading lessons offered to young students in early America. The poem was entitled "The Song of the Bee":

Buzz! Buzz! Buzz! This is the song of the bee. His legs are of yellow; a jolly good fellow, and yet a great worker is he. In days that are sunny he's getting his honey. In days that are cloudy he's making his wax. . . . Buzz! Buzz! Buzz! . . . He never gets lazy. From thistle and daisy, and weeds of the meadow some treasure he brings. Buzz! Buzz! Buzz! From morning's first light till the coming of night, he's singing and toiling the summer day through. Oh! we may get weary, and think work is dreary. 'Tis harder by far to have nothing to do.[1]

The poem praises the virtue of work. The bee — who works when its sunny or cloudy, never gets lazy, and toils from the first light until the coming of night

— is presented as a model. Like the bee, we too must toil and labor.

The poem illustrates the longstanding love affair between Americans and labor. We congratulate the hard worker. We curse the lazy worker. A strong work ethic forms the backbone of our country. But the virtue of hard work is so ingrained into our culture that it has created misunderstandings when it comes to another backbone of our country — religion. A poem by J.G. Holland, also included in Bennett's *The Book of Virtues*, illustrates how work ethic and salvation often go hand in hand. The poem is entitled "Heaven Is Not Reached at a Single Bound":

> Heaven is not reached at a single bound, but we build the ladder from which we rise, from the lowly earth to the vaulted skies, and we mount to its summit round by round. I count this thing to be grandly true: that a noble deed is a step toward God — lifting the soul from the common clod to a purer air and a broader view.[2]

On the surface, the poem teaches a genuine truth. Those who fill heaven will be people who have worked hard. But under the surface, the poem teaches something far from the truth: "*we* build the ladder by which *we* rise" and "*we* mount to its summit round by round." In other words, heaven is for those who have worked hard enough to earn it. If you want to get there, it's all up to you. *You* have to build a ladder out of good deeds. *You* have to mount its summit. Heaven waits for those who work hard enough to get in.

The idea is not a new one. In fact, since the beginning of Christianity people have bought into the idea of working our way to heaven. In the last chapter we saw how the letter of Galatians addresses that philosophy. Specifically, we saw how Paul revealed two fatal flaws in scorecard Christianity.

First, Paul says that scorecard Christianity isn't even Christianity. When we believe in scorecards, we have deserted God himself. Christianity and scorecards have nothing to do with each other.

Second, Paul says that scorecard Christianity voids the cross. If scorecard religion is valid, Jesus died for nothing. If God keeps score and allows only the high scores in, the cross happened for no reason.

The last three points in Paul's letter show why these first two points are true. Paul again takes us to the heart of the cross and its shame to bring the points home.

Flaw #3: It Ignores What Is Public

Paul's third point is this: scorecard Christianity ignores what is public. The concept is illustrated in Galatians 3:1: "You foolish Galatians! Who has bewitched you? Before your very eyes Jesus Christ was clearly portrayed as crucified."

The words "clearly portrayed" are translated from one word which literally means "placard." The word refers to a sign which gives public notice of something.[3] A modern placard might be an advertising billboard next to a highway, a "Garage Sale" sign taped to a power pole, or a "Wanted" poster hung in the post office. Here, Paul says the cross itself was a placard.

That fact has two meanings. In one sense it refers to the public knowledge of the cross. Paul wants to know how these Christians could have missed the implications of the cross for getting into heaven when it was public knowledge. Paul is like the teacher lecturing a student after the student missed an essay question on the midterm: "How could you miss that? I spent five weeks on that topic! Everybody in class knew that one!" Paul spent so much time speaking about the cross that everybody knew about it. Everybody, that is, except these scorekeeping Christians.

The cross as placard has a second meaning. It also refers to the public nature of the cross. As we've seen in previous chapters, crucifixion was the most brutal and public method of death in its day. Its disgusting nature forced people to take notice.

When I was a graduate student, I lived in apartments on the campus of Harding University Graduate School of Religion in Memphis, Tennessee. Every spring brought a strange odor to the dumpster area. As the weather warmed, the smell worsened. My first year on campus, other residents tried to ignore the smell. They were afraid of what they would find if they investigated it. But the smell was so offensive that I just couldn't ignore it. Finally, another student and I put on old clothes and jumped into the dumpster area. Rotted food, curdled milk, and rice-sized maggots greeted us. As much as we wanted to ignore the mess, its stench compelled us to attend to it.

The cross evoked the same response. You just couldn't ignore it. Its stench compelled attention. How could you ignore Philo's account of Jews in Alexandria dragged through the streets, jumped up and down on, and publicly paraded to their cross? How could you ignore 6,000 runaway slaves crucified next to a major Roman highway? How could you ignore the Roman commander Titus allowing his soldiers to nail Jewish bodies in different postures on the walls of Jerusalem? The cross of Christ was no different. It was a public and disgrace-filled spectacle. Paul implies that when we rely on the merit of our own good deeds, it's like walking by the cross and pretending it isn't there. Scorecard religion ignores what is public.

Flaw #4: It Requires Perfection

Fourth, scorecard Christianity requires a perfect score. We tend to believe that scorecard Christianity operates like school. As long as you make A's, B's, and C's, you get to walk at graduation. As long as you score between 70 and 100 on your finals, you're secure. But in Galatians 5:1-3, Paul says that if you choose scorecard Christianity, only a perfect score will be accepted:

> It is for freedom that Christ has set us free. Stand firm, then, and do not let yourselves be burdened again by a yoke of slavery. Mark my words! I, Paul, tell you that if you let yourselves be circumcised, Christ will be of no value to you at all. Again I declare to every man who lets himself be circumcised that he is obligated to obey the whole law.

Paul warns his readers that if they gave in to one small part of this philosophy — circumcision — they were obligated to give in to the whole thing. In a similar way, if we give in to just one part of scorecard thinking, we must give in to the whole thing. We don't get to choose what requirements go on the scorecard and what score it takes on each of the requirements. It's an all or nothing card. We either do every activity with a perfect score, or we can forget the whole thing.

Under the banner of scorecards, we must *stop* every bad habit and action. From insensitive comments to our spouse, to insincere worship to our God — it all has to stop. Lust, lying, and laziness must die. We must *start* every good habit and action listed in the Bible. From helping the poor, to heartfelt worship — it all has to start. Compassion, character, and conviction must live.

And not only does the bad have to stop and the good have to start if we use scorecards, but the bad has to stay stopped every single day and the good has to keep on every single day. One bad day, and it's all for nothing. One slip up, one mistake, one foul up, and we can forget it. One lie, one curse word, one word of anger, one song in worship that we don't really mean, and we can kiss heaven good-bye.

Paul calls that kind of religion slavery. You don't have to live it very long to realize how right he is. Since scorecard Christianity requires a perfect score, it is slavery, pure and simple.

Flaw #5: It Attempts to Finish the Finished

Paul's final point brings the previous four points together. His fifth point is that scorecard Christianity attempts to complete what is already complete:

> I would like to learn just one thing from you: Did you receive the Spirit by observing the law, or by believing what you heard? Are you so foolish? After beginning

with the Spirit, are you now trying to attain your goal by human effort (Gal 3:2-3)?

For Paul, the Holy Spirit is the greatest symbol of God's gift to Christians. There is no higher privilege than possession of the Spirit of God. It is a guarantee that the possessor is going to heaven. Here, Paul sarcastically asks that, having gained this prized possession without scores, will they get the rest by human effort? Literally, Paul asks if they are going to "complete" or "finish" the goal (of salvation) by external means like "good deeds." These Christians were guilty of trying to complete their salvation by adding to what God gave them with their own works.

It's not that these Christians thought they didn't need the cross. They just thought it didn't quite finish the job. Many times that's how we view the cross. It is an important and necessary part of our salvation. On our scorecard, it makes the biggest single score. But we see it as only part of the score necessary to get into heaven.

For many, the cross is similar to the Apollo space project highlighted by the 1996 movie *Apollo 13* starring Tom Hanks. The Apollo project had one main goal: to launch humans into space, put them onto the moon, and return them back to earth. Apollo flights were launched by the three stage Saturn V rocket, which developed 7.5 million pounds of thrust at liftoff. At launch, the total assembly stood 363 feet high and weighed more than 3,000 tons. The Saturn V rocket provided the thrust to get the entire packaged off the launch pad and into space. Once in space, however, astronauts still had to perform a delicate docking maneuver with the lunar module, thrust to the moon, land the lunar module on the moon, blast off from the moon, rejoin the command ship, thrust back to earth, and splash down nine days after take off.[4]

Often we view the cross like the first stage of that Saturn V rocket. The cross is the 7.5 million pounds of thrust which hurtles us toward heaven. We know we need it. We understand that heaven would be out of reach without it. Yet we tend to think that the benefits of the cross stop well short of heaven. It's up to us to dock with the lunar module, land on the moon, thrust back to earth, and perform the careful splash down. The cross gives us a boost, but we still have a ways to go. The cross gives us a good starting score, but there are still points to gain before heaven becomes a reality.

Paul's point is that the cross is not just a booster rocket for part of the trip. It is the trip. Everything that needed to be done was done at the cross. The entire score was gained by that cross. When we become Christians, God hands us scorecards where every blank has already been filled. The total has been tallied and it reads 100%. Before we ever take a merit-earning step, our scorecard is filled with perfect scores.

Every time we slip into scorecard thinking, however, we imply that Jesus didn't do enough. When we sin and then do a sacrificial act the next day to make up for it, we imply that Jesus didn't suffer enough. When we go to bed feeling that things have never been better between us and God because we just gave $50 to a poor family, we imply that Jesus needed to hang on the cross a little longer. When we answer the question "Why do you think you'll go to heaven?" by listing our church attendance and the middle school class we teach, we imply that a little more blood needed to flow from Jesus' body. These acts shout that Jesus' humiliation was insufficient; the stench wasn't strong enough; the victory wasn't complete.

But Paul states that the cross is all that's necessary. On the cross, Jesus made the perfect score so we wouldn't have to. The reason the cross could score so perfectly is that nothing could best it. When Philo wrote of the atrocities visited upon the Jews in Alexandria, he put it in this way: "[They] were arrested, scourged, tortured, and after all these outrages, which were all their bodies could make room for, the final punishment kept in reserve for them was the cross."[5] Once someone was crucified, there was nothing left you could do to them that hadn't been done. Once Jesus was crucified, there was nothing left we could do to get into heaven that hadn't already been done. Scorecard Christianity attempts to complete what is already complete.

Trusting the Savior v. Tallying the Score

Thus Paul says the only real way to be "justified" is by faith:

> We who are Jews by birth and not "Gentile sinners" know that a man is not justified by observing the law, but by faith in Jesus Christ. So we, too, have put our faith in Christ Jesus that we may be justified by faith in Christ and not by observing the law because by observing the law, no one will be justified (Gal 2:15-16).

> You are all sons of God through faith in Christ Jesus, for all of you who were baptized into Christ have clothed yourselves with Christ (3:26-27).

Heaven is gained not by faith in our works, but by faith in *his* works. Faith is simply the belief that the cross was enough. It is a trust that Jesus did everything necessary for us to be in the clear. It is a conviction that our performance cannot earn our salvation.

And that's not always an easy thing to believe. William Willimon tells of Michael Green who used to host social parties to reach non-Christians. As people ate and drank, Christians tried to steer conversations to spiritual matters. During one party, a woman leaned over to Michael in the midst of his discussion about Jesus and said, "You know, I don't believe any of this."

Michael replied, "Yeah, I know. But wouldn't you like to?"

Tears began welling up in her eyes.[6]

It's almost too good to believe. Even as a Christian, it may be hard to have faith in a system like this. But Paul begs that we would. Paul pulls us back to the disgrace of the cross and asks us to believe not in what we can do, but in what Jesus has already done.

Endnotes

1. Marian Douglas, "The Song of the Bee," in *The Book of Virtues* by William Bennett, (New York: Simon & Schuster, 1993), 349-350.

2. J.G. Holland, "Heaven Is Not Reached in a Single Bound," *The Book of Virtues*, William Bennett, ed. (New York: Simon & Schuster, 1993), 415.

3. "προγράφω," Walter Bauer, *A Greek-English Lexicon of the New*

Testament and Other Early Christian Literature, translated by William F. Arndt and F. Wilbur Gingrich (Chicago: University of Chicago Press, 1979), 704.

4. "Rocket," and "Space Exploration," in *The New Columbia Encyclopedia* 4th edition, ed. by William Harris & Judith Levey (New York: Columbia University Press, 1975): 2338-2339; 2579-2581.

5. Philo, *In Flaccum*, 72.

6. Steve Brown, Haddon Robinson, William Willimon, *A Voice in the Wilderness*, Mastering Ministry's Pressure Points (Portland, OR: Multnomah Books, 1993): 88-89.

Study Questions

1. The chapter begins with illustrations showing a misunderstanding concerning hard work and heaven. What is the real relationship between the two?

2. Share a time in your life when you or someone you knew tried to ignore something public (e.g., the author's experience with trash in Memphis). What circumstances or attitudes make it possible for you or others to ignore the cross and its implications concerning our freedom from scorekeeping?

3. How does the fact that scorecard Christianity requires perfect scores decrease the appeal of this type of thinking?

4. List twenty sins you would have to perfectly stop, and twenty virtues you would have to perfectly start in order to get into heaven under scorecard Christianity. Share how such a system truly is slavery. Have you personally experienced that kind of slavery? Explain.

5. Have you ever tried to make it up to God for a sin by doing something sacrificial the next day, or felt good about your relationship with God because of some good deed like church attendance or gifts to the poor? Explain. Is there a place in the Christian life for feeling good about doing good things?

6. How can the cross score such a perfect score and so completely achieve what we cannot?

7. Do you find the concepts in this chapter and the previous chapter hard to believe? Why?

THE CROSS

Part Three

Part Three

Living on the Cross
A Life of Service

The cross serves not only as the paradigm for true celebration; it also serves as the paradigm for true service. Those called to dance under the cross are also called to die on the cross. Under the cross we are freed from the burden of slavery. On the cross we are yoked with the bonds of service. Service to God. Service to others.

The cross-carrier and his followers used the cross as the ultimate illustration of the demands of following God and loving others. Both in our relationship with God, and in our relationship with neighbor, the cross is the only standard by which we can measure our behavior. As the one who first died on it, we are called to die on it again and again. The next two chapters explore the finality of this death and how it affects our walk with God and with those we love.

✠ 6 ✠

The Cross Holds No Imposters

In *Christianity Today*, George Brushaber described attending a murder mystery dinner theater where diners would be drawn into the cast and challenged to identify the murderer hidden among the professional actors. It promised to be an exciting evening. The promise, however, proved to be pathetic. The servers rarely served. The first course killed appetites. The diners shanghaied into minor roles failed miserably. And even the professional cast barely passed for actors.

Later, Brushaber summarized the evening with one word — "fake." The chef poorly imitated gourmet cuisine. The waiters were imposters. The actors (must have) carried false credentials. The entire evening was fake.[1]

Most of us can relate to Brushaber's frustration with imposters. And sadly, some of us have played the role of imposter. We have claimed to be what we weren't. For the sake of a kiss, we claimed that our love was true and forever. To get that first job, we falsified previous work experience. There are times when we fake our role on the stage of life. We speak lines which aren't ours.

But deep down, few of us want to live as fakes. We want to speak the lines written specifically for us. We want to play our part with genuineness. Nowhere is that desire more intense than in our life as Christians. Few of us want to be imitation Christians. Most of us want to be authentic Christians. We want to live what we believe. We want congruity between who we claim to be and who we really are. But what does it mean to live authentically as a Christian? What test can identify imposter-like attitudes in our Christianity?

In the last three chapters we saw how the disgrace of the cross sheds light on what it means to live *under* the cross — in a life of celebration. We celebrate because the cross has done everything necessary for us to be in heaven. In this chapter and the next, we see how the disgrace of the cross sheds light on what it means to live *on* the cross — in a life of service. The cross alone stands as the symbol for authentic Christian living. Only those willing to die on the cross themselves can carry the label "Christian" with any integrity. Our presence on a cross is the test of our authenticity.

In this chapter, we'll explore the cross-death we are called to in our relationship with Jesus. In the next chapter we'll explore that death as it relates to our relationships with others.

Cost-Free Christianity

Large crowds were traveling with Jesus, and turning to them he said: "If anyone comes to me and does not hate his father and mother, his wife and children, his

94

brothers and sisters — yes, even his own life — he cannot be my disciple. And anyone who does not carry his cross and follow me cannot be my disciple.

Suppose one of you wants to build a tower. Will he not first sit down and estimate the cost to see if he has enough money to complete it? For if he lays the foundation and is not able to finish it, everyone who sees it will ridicule him, saying 'This fellow began to build and was not able to finish.'

Or suppose a king is about to go to war against another king. Will he not first sit down and consider whether he is able with ten thousand men to oppose the one coming against him with twenty thousand? If he is not able, he will send a delegation while the other is still a long way off and will ask for terms of peace. In the same way, any of you who does not give up everything he has cannot be my disciple" (Luke 14:25-33).

Before this cutting speech in Luke's gospel, Jesus had issued few demands on the crowds around him. They received miracles from this master magician, cures from this daring doctor, and insight from this talented teacher. After such a lengthy period of receiving, it was probably easy for them to believe that following Jesus simply involved getting what Jesus gave. Luke doesn't specifically tell us that this crowd believed such lies. But Jesus' abrupt change of topic from the cuisine of a heavenly banquet in Luke 14:1-24, to the cost of being a disciple in Luke 14:25-35, and the harsh tone in which Jesus delivers this speech indicate that the crowd probably did have such misunderstandings. It is likely that Jesus' fans believed that a relationship with him was more about consuming than contributing.

It would be easy for us to feel the same after the concepts raised in the last three chapters. Those chapters proclaimed that there is nothing we can do to get into heaven that Jesus hasn't already done for us. Thus it is tempting to believe that a relationship with Christ involves waiting for him to do even more for us. Like the crowd, we may envision Christianity as all take and no give.

Through the centuries, this has been a common misunderstanding of Christianity. The crowd of Luke 14:25-35 wasn't the last to be swayed by such a deception. In the 1400s, a priest named Thomas à Kempis accused the crowds of his day with these words:

> Jesus has many who love His Kingdom in Heaven, but few who bear His Cross. He has many who desire comfort, but few who desire suffering. He finds many to share His feast, but few His fasting. All desire to rejoice with Him, but few are willing to suffer for His sake. Many follow Jesus to the Breaking of Bread, but few to the drinking of the Cup of His Passion. Many admire his miracles, but few follow Him in the humiliation of His Cross.[2]

In the late 1980s, the well-known researcher George Gallup, Jr. turned to the crowds of his day with the same challenge:

> We boast Christianity as our faith, but many of us have not bothered to learn basic facts of this religion. Many of us dutifully attend church, but this act appears to have made us no less likely than our unchurched brethren to engage in unethical behavior. We say we are Christians, but sometimes we do not show much love

toward those who do not share our particular religious perspective. We say we rejoice in the good news that Jesus brought, but we are often strangely reluctant to share the gospel with others. . . . We say we are believers, but perhaps we are only assenters.[3]

It's always been tempting to believe that a relationship with Jesus is demand-free. We enjoy the benefits of his sacrifice, but we need make no sacrifice of our own. After all, heaven is already ours. What good would any sacrifice on our part have? Yet in the cutting words in Luke 14, Jesus states that sacrifice is the primary quality demanded by our relationship with him.

Costly Miscalculations

The issue in this text is resources. The two parables tucked into the middle of the speech illustrate the importance of resources. In the first parable, the goal is to build a tower — probably a watchtower that a property owner might construct in his vineyard to watch for animals and thieves. Jesus states that there are two paths to that goal. One path is the path of immediate construction. Without some forethought, however, materials run short and the tower stands unfinished. The second path is the path of careful calculation. Forethought is given as to the resources needed to accomplish the goal. Once they are calculated, the tower can be built to completion.

In the second parable, the goal is to go to war against a rival king. As with the first parable, there are two paths to this goal. One path is immediate war. Without some forethought, however, the king with 20,000 will annihilate the one with 10,000. The second path is the path of careful calculation. Forethought is given as to the resources needed to accomplish the goal. Once calculated, the king with 10,000 will realize his shortfall and can send an ambassador to sue for peace.

Jesus uses the two parables to show that there are also resources needed to authentically follow him — or in the words of Jesus, to be a "disciple." Jesus uses the word "disciple" three times to describe one who has a true relationship with him. A builder needs certain resources to build a tower. A king needs certain resources to engage in battle. A Christian needs certain resources to be a disciple. Jesus lists three specific resources which a genuine disciple must have.

Three Sincere Sacrifices

Hating Loved Ones

First, according to Luke 14:26, an authentic Christian needs hate. Like me, you're probably tempted to tone this word down. Hate is what racists and murderers possess, not Christians. But to tone the word down would be to pull the plug on Jesus' argument. Jesus intends this word to shock.

Jesus doesn't mean real Christians mistreat father, mother, wife, children, brothers and sisters. The same Jesus also said that we are to love our enemies. Surely we are to love our families as well. Jesus' point here becomes clear when he applies the word not only to our families, but to our own lives as well. In as strong a way as possible, Jesus states that having a real relationship with him means hating yourself and your interests so

that you can honor him and his interests. Jesus'
agenda for our jobs, families, and moral lives must so
overshadow our agenda that we can truly say we hate
our agenda. Hatred for self in the sense of renouncing
all relationships and activities which keep us from following Christ is a necessary resource.

Saying Farewell to Finances

Another resource is found in Luke 14:33. Jesus literally describes this resource as the ability to "say farewell
to that which we own". Jesus is not equating owning
things with insincere Christianity. But he is saying that
authentic Christianity involves the willingness to give
up the use or ownership of any and all possessions if
that act will help us serve him.

Climbing on a Cross

While these two resources are more than we could
expect, they are lost in the shadow of the third resource.
With the third resource, Jesus makes authentic Christianity a deadly proposition. Perhaps the most shocking
resource for a real relationship with Christ is the one
listed in Luke 14:27. Jesus says that those wanting to
follow him must carry a cross. Genuine Christians,
Jesus says, will die disgracefully and painfully.

Plutarch, an ancient author, helps illuminate this
final resource. In one of his books, he discusses whether
or not criminals ever truly get punished for their crimes.
To prove that crime is generally followed by punishment, he gives an example from his day: ". . . every
criminal who goes to execution must carry his own
cross on his back . . . ."[4] Plutarch says that a cross on

one's back was a guarantee of punishment. Once the criminal picked up the cross, unspeakable death was certain. But Jesus says that the cross and its punishment are not only for criminals. They are for Christians.

To make sure we grasp the fundamental necessity of these three resources, Jesus speaks of them more than once. They appear earlier in Luke 9:18-26:

> Once when Jesus was praying in private and his disciples were with him, he asked them, "Who do the crowds say I am?"
>
> They replied, "Some say John the Baptist; others say Elijah; and still others, that one of the prophets of long ago has come back to life."
>
> "But what about you?" he asked. "Who do you say I am?"
>
> Peter answered, "The Christ of God."
>
> Jesus strictly warned them not to tell this to anyone. And he said, "The Son of Man must suffer many things and be rejected by the elders, chief priests and teachers of the law, and he must be killed and on the third day be raised to life."
>
> Then he said to them all: "If anyone would come after me, he must deny himself and take up his cross daily and follow me. For whoever wants to save his life will lose it, but whoever loses his life for me will save it. What good is it for a man to gain the whole world, and yet lose or forfeit his very self? If anyone is ashamed of me and my words, the Son of Man will be ashamed of him when he comes in his glory and in the glory of the Father and of the holy angels."

In Luke 14 the issue was resources. Here the issue is definition. In the first part of this discussion, the stated question is "Who is Jesus?" Several wrong definitions are given before the correct definition is given by Peter. Jesus then qualifies that definition with one of his own. Who is Jesus? Jesus is someone who will climb on a cross and die.

In the second part of the discussion, the question changes. Instead of "Who is Jesus?", the question is "Who is a Christian?" And Jesus again points to three things.

First, in Luke 9:24, Jesus points to hatred or the giving up of life. Jesus implies that a meaningful life is only found when it is lost — lost for Christ. The definition of a real Christian is someone who gives life up for Christ.

Second, in Luke 9:26, Jesus points to possessions. "Gaining the whole world" is the language of wealth. Jesus implies that real riches are found only in the loss of riches. The definition of a real Christian is one for whom wealth means little. Thus, those with a true relationship with Christ will be defined by a desire to lose their lives and their luxuries for Christ.

Third, and more importantly, Jesus points to the cross to define a real Christian. In Luke 9:22, Jesus shows that being a real Messiah means going to the cross. Similarly, in Luke 9:23, Jesus shows that being a real Christian also means going to the cross.

Deadly Discipleship

Cross carrying stands at the center of both texts. Think of all the images Jesus could have used from his life to illustrate authentic Christianity. He could have described it in terms of his incarnation — serving people in a form with which those people can relate. He could have described it in terms of his miraculous ministry — allowing the power of God to work through us to touch others. He could have used the image of his preaching ministry to define discipleship — telling people the news of God. He could have used his own concern for the poor and children as a resource for discipleship. But Jesus chose an image from his last hours — the image of carrying a cross and dying on a cross. That is what real discipleship is all about. And that was not just a resource for leaders. It isn't the definition for saints. It is what anyone wanting to call himself a Christian must do. All authentic Christians carry crosses.

In the ears of Jesus' listeners, that concept would have evoked an emotional response. They would have known stories like the one concerning Antiochus Epiphanes who invaded Judea in 169 BC. Jesus could have stated his point using the story: "Let me explain what you must do to follow me. Do you remember when Epiphanes punished our families when we refused to stop circumcising our sons? Do you remember how he took the fathers and whipped them and mutilated them? Do you remember how they groaned as he punctured their skin while nailing them to crosses, and then forced them to witness the strangling of their wives and sons? And do you remember the final act? The sons who had been strangled were hung from the necks of the fathers on the crosses. That's what you have to endure if you want to follow me. That's what it means to be a real Christian."[5]

With this image, Jesus may have certainly had actual martyrdom in mind. Some of those following Jesus would face real crosses themselves. Yet Jesus had much more in mind than physical death. Surrounding the image of cross-carrying with words about self-hatred and renunciation of possessions shows that Jesus envisioned a broader application. Cross carrying implies a complete death to self in the daily activities of life.

Cross carrying does not refer to an inconvenience like an unruly child or a demanding boss. It refers to a decision to place Jesus and his desires immeasurably far above our own. As John Stott puts it in his book *The Cross of Christ*, "Our 'cross' then, is not an irritable husband or a cantankerous wife. It is instead the symbol of death to the self."[6]

In fact, in Luke 9:23, Jesus calls this a daily death. In Jesus' day no one climbed on a cross more than once. One time did it — every time. But Jesus says the demands of discipleship are so profound that real Christians must endure disgraceful crucifixion every day.

The word "daily" indicates that this sacrifice is not a onetime decision. It might seem that a call for sacrifice this great could only happen once in life. A boss calls for dishonesty at work and you quit your job to keep your faith. A proposed law violates Christian freedom and you spend your life savings fighting the proposition. A third-world country dies from lack of food and faith, so you leave your family and fiance to alleviate the suffering. Such cross-bearing sacrifice must surely come only once in a while.

But Jesus says this sacrifice comes every day. Every day we are called to endure symbolically what those fathers endured physically at the hands of Epiphanes. It's not that two or three times this year we will be asked to pay the ultimate price for our faith. Jesus implies we will be asked that every day. It's not just in the jungles of Africa or the streets of the former Soviet Union where cross-carrying will be called for. It's at home with our kids and spouse. It's in the office with coworkers. It's at school in chemistry class. It's alone at night. Even the most common situations will call for the most uncommon sacrifice.

Jesus is not saying that we can't take care of ourselves. Neither is he forbidding joy and pleasure. But as graphically as possible, Jesus is saying that every day must be faced with a willingness to completely kill self-interest if it will help us serve Christ.

Second Rate Christianity

In Luke 14:34-35, Jesus says that this willingness to die is not an option:

> Salt is good, but if it loses its saltiness, how can it be made salty again? It is fit neither for the soil nor for the manure pile; it is thrown out.

This mini-parable is one of authenticity. Salt adds flavor to the most bland of foods. But if it lost its flavor, the result would be disastrous. Even second-rate salt in Jesus' day could be used for fertilizing the soil, or regulating the decay rate in manure piles. But if salt lost all its saltiness, it would become useless. It would wear the name "salt," but would have none of the defining qualities of salt.

In the same way, someone who claims to be a Christian yet is unwilling to die totally and disgracefully to self is useless. He would wear the name "Christian," but would have none of the defining qualities of a Christian.

In Luke 9:26 Jesus makes a similar statement. Those who are ashamed of putting self to death in order to serve Christ, will find Christ ashamed of them when he returns. Perhaps with a play on words from the disgrace of crucifixion, Jesus says there will be no greater disgrace than to find yourself off the cross when he returns. In contrast to the thought of his day, real disgrace is not found on a cross. For a Christian, real disgrace is found off the cross. The cross holds no imposters.

Endnotes

1. George K. Brushaber, "Get Real," *Christianity Today* (October 24, 1994): 15.

2. Thomas à Kempis, *The Imitation of Christ*, Penguin Books, Translated by Leo Sherley-Price (Cox & Wyman Ltd, Reading, 1979), 83.

3. George Gallup, Jr., & George O'Connell, *Who Do Americans Say That I Am?* (Philadelphia: Westminster, 1986): 88-89.

4. Plutarch, *On the Delays of Divine Vengeance*, Book vii, 554B 9.

5. Josephus, *Jewish Antiquities*, 12.256.

6. John Stott, *The Cross of Christ* (Downers Grove, IL: Inter-Varsity Press, 1986), 279.

Study Questions

1. Have there been times in your life when you felt like you were an imposter in your Christian life? Explain.

2. Kempis and Gallup provide proof of people viewing Christianity as all take and no give. What are some other modern indications that people view Christianity this way?

3. Do you find yourself sharing the view of Christianity held by the people described by Kempis and Gallup? Explain.

4. What relationship in your life do you need to apply "hate" to?

5. In what ways do you need to change your attitude toward and use of finances and possessions to be more authentic?

6. Why does Jesus use a cross, instead of his incarnation or preaching ministry, as the symbol for authentic discipleship?

7. What is the difference between carrying a cross and simply enduring an inconvenience?

8. Taking each of the major areas of your life (home, work, school, and play), describe what it means for you to carry a cross in each area.

9. How has your understanding of what it means to be authentic in your walk with God changed as a result of this chapter?

10. How do you reconcile this chapter with the previous chapters?

7

Climbing Up to Better Relationships

Dr. Ralph Underwager of the Institute for Psychological Therapies in Northfield, Minnesota, who also identifies himself as a theologian, made this statement in a November 1993 *Voices* magazine: "I believe that God's will is that we have absolute freedom. No conditions, no contingencies."[1] This statement illustrates one of the two most common misconceptions about Christianity. On the one hand, many wrongly believe that God's will is for us to have no freedom, and that only by perfectly keeping his conditions and contingencies do we earn our way to heaven. As earlier chapters have shown, however, the cross and its disgrace deflate that misconception. On the other hand, many wrongly believe that God's will is for us to have no conditions and contingencies. Since our performance cannot earn our seat in heaven, it is tempting to believe performance no longer matters.

The last chapter illustrated the perversity of this

second misconception. We saw how Jesus used the cross and its disgrace to show the conditions and contingencies which are part of an authentic relationship with him. We saw that we are called to a life on the cross — a life of service. A real relationship with Christ involves a total death to self. In this chapter, we'll see how the cross also illustrates the conditions necessary in another area — our relationships with the people in our lives. As we've done before, we'll again spend time in the book of Galatians to explore the practical implications of the cross.

How to Kill a Good Relationship

> You, my brothers, were called to be free. But do not use your freedom to indulge the sinful nature; rather, serve one another in love (Gal 5:13).

Up to this point in Galatians, Paul has been surveying the broad slopes of grace. He has explored grace's expanse for four and a half chapters. But after such a lengthy investigation of grace, Paul knows he will easily be misunderstood. Based on his words above, it appears that his fear has become reality.

Having rappelled with Paul across the slopes of grace and freedom, some of Paul's readers are now using freedom to justify faulty behavior. Literally, they are using grace as a "pretext" for living with no conditions or contingencies. The word for "pretext" originally referred to a base of operations, or the resources needed for a journey.[2] If you were to climb a tall mountain, you would use this word to describe the base camp from which you started. If you created a list of items which you needed for the trip, this word would describe the most crucial items on the list. Some of Paul's readers are using their freedom from having to do things to earn heaven as the base from which they start on a long and wrong journey. They carry freedom as a resource to propel them down a dangerous path. As proof of his fear, Paul illustrates the journey that some of his readers have already taken in the name of grace:

> If you keep on biting and devouring each other, watch out or you will be destroyed by each other. . . . The acts of the sinful nature are obvious: sexual immorality, impurity and debauchery; idolatry and witchcraft; hatred, discord, jealousy, fits of rage, selfish ambition, dissensions, factions and envy; drunkenness, orgies, and the like. I warn you, as I did before, that those who live like this will not inherit the kingdom of God. . . . Let us not become conceited, provoking and envying each other (Gal 5:15,19-21,26).

These Christians weren't misusing freedom to lie their way to better jobs or to steal money from banks. They were misusing freedom to destroy their relationships. Their base of operations led them down a path which believed that having a relationship with another person simply meant taking what you wanted from that person.

With the phrase "biting and devouring each other," Paul raises the image of a pack of animals who fight so ferociously that they annihilate one another. They so aggressively assert their freedom to harm others that they literally devour them.

That violent image might cause us to feel better about Paul's words. After all, most of us have never stated out loud what Dr. Underwager did. Most of us have never used Christian freedom as the silverware with which we devour another person. Yet before we begin to feel self-righteous, we must notice the details which follow the first gruesome image. Paul shows us that this tendency to misuse freedom can affect our relationships in much more subtle ways.

In the verses quoted above, Paul lists fifteen actions which commonly result from a misunderstanding of the celebration allowed under the cross. At least eight of those actions involve relationships. When we refuse to live on the cross, we can expect these eight diseases to infect our relationships.

First, Paul says that we often use God's free love for us to freely hate others. The word "hate" means enmity and hostility.[3] It is the opposite of love and forgiveness. This word describes the husband who accepts his unfaithful wife back into his life, but never truly forgives her. The word describes the two families who sit on opposite sides of a church auditorium because of a conflict between them years ago. The conflict is long gone but the feelings are as fresh as ever.

Second, Paul shows that Christians often justify discord in their relationships by pointing to the cross. The word "discord" refers to strife, quarreling, or contention with others.[4] It describes that high school student who knows what buttons to push to get the teacher upset. It refers to the wife who always has to have the last word, and demands that her word is always the right word.

Third, jealousy can rise in the relationships of Christians who believe that since Jesus paid it all on the cross, there are no more prices to be paid. "Jealousy" refers to that unfriendly feeling you get toward someone because of his/her success in some area.[5] When your life is full of troubles and you talk to an old friend on the phone who seems to stumble into the best circumstances, this word describes that gnawing at your heart. When the coworker who couldn't finish a report without your help gets recognition for a project you did by yourself, you feel this word.

Fourth, rage is a real possibility in the lives of Christians who misunderstand grace. This word simply refers to anger.[6] This is the parent who repeatedly tells her child not to do something. When the child disobeys for the fifth time, the parent angrily smacks the child and pushes her against the wall. This is the child whose eighty-year-old parent suffers from Alzheimer's. The parent forgets names, places, and faces. He can't feed himself and often spills food on the adult child. After a particularly frustrating episode, the child pushes the parent away and storms from the room.

Fifth, those who only read the first four chapters of Galatians might allow ambition to color their relationships. This word refers to someone who is self-seeking.[7] It is the parent who works so hard to get ahead at work that she loses a family in the process. It is the church member who fights for a certain way of doing things not out of biblical convictions, but out of a desire to have things his way.

Sixth and seventh, Paul lists dissensions and factions as qualities which infect relationships when Christians don't grasp the serious nature of discipleship. These words refer to people who cause divisions or who create sects or parties.[8] The words could refer to someone who causes division by distinguishing between certain kinds of people. This is the business owner who refuses to serve the poor. This is the student who won't sit next to someone with mental or physical handicaps. This is the Christian who accepts only those who line up with her list of opinions and preferences.

Eighth, Paul warns that envy often invades relationships when people live off the cross. This word describes that feeling you get toward someone who has what you want.[9] It is the computer owner who dives into depression every time his friend upgrades his computer. It is the struggling couple who cuts off contact with their friends whose marriage is dynamic and fulfilling.

Finally, Paul lists two other characteristics of the relationships of Christians who confuse liberty with license. "Conceit" describes the guy who thinks he's an expert in every field and doesn't mind telling you how to do everything you do. "Provoke" is the girl who won't put the past to rest and constantly reminds her boyfriend of his previous mistakes.

According to Paul, this is the inevitable journey our relationships will take if we believe that Jesus' sacrifice means no sacrifice on our part. We may not start here. But our journey will end here. The minute we entertain the idea that Christianity is cost free, the disease of hate and selfishness begins to incubate in our relationships. Over weeks and months, the glow of healthy relationships will fade into the gray of dying relationships. The disease will run its course, and the relationship will die.

Disease Control for Relationships

Knowing this, Paul reminds us that Christian freedom is not freedom to hurt others. Instead, it is freedom to serve others:

> . . . rather, serve one another in love. The entire law is summed up in a single command: "Love your neighbor as yourself."
>
> But the fruit of the Spirit is love, joy, peace, patience, kindness, goodness, faithfulness, gentleness and self-control. Against such things there is no law (Gal 5:13b-14,22-23).

It is important not to see this call to serve and love as just another law to follow in order to get to heaven. Those who had infiltrated this church were saying that the best way to cure bad relationships was with a stiff dose of law. Prescribe a list of rigorous do's and do not's, and the relationships will shape up. But Paul says that we have been freed from that kind of system. Prescriptions of law will only worsen the relationship.

Yet Paul also affirms that the call for service and love in relationships is a serious call. Paradoxically, we have been freed from slavery to law, but we have been freed to the slavery to others. We are free to serve.

To show just how sacrificial that service to others is, Paul points to the cross: "Those who belong to Christ Jesus have crucified the sinful nature with its passions and desires (Gal 5:24)." Paul raises the cross to illustrate how far we must be willing to go in our relationships with others. Our base of operations is the cross. Every journey we take with others must start with our climbing on a cross. Our primary resource for relationships is crucifixion. Instead of crucifying others, we are called to crucify ourselves. Instead of carrying a grudge, we are to carry a cross. The cross is the medication which immunizes relationships against the diseases of hatred and selfishness.

In the verse above, Paul envisions an already/not yet crucifixion. In one sense, we have already been crucified to the selfish passions and desires which infect relationships. At baptism, that part of us was crucified. But in another sense, we are not yet fully crucified. We constantly reapply crucifixion in our daily relationships. As we relate to our spouse, friend, coworker, neighbor, and stranger, we apply our previous crucifixion to the present relationship.

What we crucify is called the "sinful nature" in the NIV. Literally, Paul uses the word "flesh." "Flesh" doesn't refer to our skin with its acne and blemishes. It refers to that fundamental part of our humanity which wants its own way. And Paul says this self-seeking part of us struggles with the God-seeking Spirit within us:

> For the sinful nature desires what is contrary to the Spirit, and the Spirit what is contrary to the sinful nature. They are in conflict with each other, so that you do not do what you want (Gal 5:17).

Our natural tendency is to do things our way — especially when it comes to relationships. But Paul says that tendency must be eliminated so that the Spirit can have his way. Paul doesn't just want that self-seeking tendency to be mildly toned down. Paul isn't suggesting that the murderer work down to just being a hater, and the hater work down to just being a disliker. Neither is

Paul suggesting that this quality which infects relationships be temporarily killed for special occasions. He
doesn't want us to be a teddy bear at home and church
and a tiger at work. Paul calls for a permanent crucifixion to our self-seeking tendencies. In every relationship,
we are to climb on a cross and die.

Death Illustrated

In 76 BC, an ancient author named Cicero was elected
quaestor. During his year in office, he was sent to Sicily
to work on the governor's staff. He favorably impressed
the Sicilians because of his diligence and honesty. In 73
BC, a senator named Gaius Verres became governor of
Sicily and held that position for three years. Verres was
thoroughly shameless and unscrupulous in using his
position to enrich himself. By the time he left Sicily,
many of its inhabitants were destitute.

The Sicilians sent a delegation to Rome and brought
Verres to trial. Cicero was asked to speak for the prosecution. He gathered a mass of evidence against Verres.
Part of the evidence was Verres' actions towards a Roman
citizen named Gavius of Consa. Normally a Roman citizen like Gavius was exempt from the disgrace of crucifixion. In spite of that widely accepted law, however,
Verres ordered Gavius stripped, tied, and whipped. The
man protested that he was a Roman citizen and that he
had served in the Roman army. But Verres refused to
listen. Verres then ordered him to be whipped many
times all over his body. The whole time Gavius suffered,
all he said was "I am a Roman citizen." Cicero writes the
end of this account in these words:

117

The Cross: Saved by the Shame of It All

> . . . Verres ordered his staff to make for this poor tor-
> mented man a cross. That's right, a cross! . . . Gentle-
> men of the jury, this was the only cross ever set up in
> the part of Messana that over looks the straits. Verres
> chose this spot, with its view of Italy, deliberately so
> that Gavius, as he died in pain and agony, might recog-
> nize that the narrow straits marked the boundary
> between slavery and freedom, and so that Italy might
> see her own son hanging there, suffering the most horri-
> ble punishment ever inflicted on slaves. To put a Roman
> citizen in chains is wrong. To flog him is a crime. To
> execute him is almost parricide. And what shall I call
> crucifixion? So abominable a deed can find no word
> adequate enough to describe it.[10]

The most horrible punishment ever inflicted on slaves.

So abominable a deed that no word can adequately describe it.

Paul says such a deed must be done in our daily relationships. In every relationship, we are called to endure what Gavius endured. We are called to a disgraceful death to self.

When your unfaithful spouse returns, your anger must return to the cross.

When you feel like pushing someone's buttons, push yourself up a cross instead.

When that coworker gets recognition for your work, it's time for you to recognize your need for the cross.

If you feel like nailing your child, nail yourself to a cross.

If you fight to get your way just because it's your way, you need to find your way back to the cross.

If you create divisions by rejecting those who aren't like you, its time to be united to your cross.

When you want to get that classmate back for ridiculing, get back on the cross.

That's the standard to which we are called. That's the sacrifice we must be willing to make.

How about a Hand?

Paul's prescription for healthy relationships isn't easy. Self-crucifixion is difficult, if not impossible. In fact, it is impossible without divine help. That's why Paul shows that our resource for relationships is not just crucifixion, but resurrection. We not only have to die on a cross. We get to live through the Spirit:

> So I say, live by the Spirit, and you will not gratify the desires of the sinful nature. . . . the fruit of the Spirit is love, joy, peace, patience, kindness, goodness, faithfulness, gentleness and self control. . . . Since we live by the Spirit, let us keep in step with the Spirit (Gal 5:16, 22-23,25).

As our life evaporates on that cross, it returns through the Spirit. The Spirit bears fruit in our relationships. The Spirit empowers us to die this real death in every relationship. Note that most of the fruit borne by the Spirit has to do with relationship issues.

But the Spirit doesn't do all the work for us. We are to "keep in step with the Spirit." The Spirit leads the way, pointing out new directions and beckoning us to follow. But it is up to us to follow. In every relationship, we can choose to follow the Spirit and accept the Spirit's help. Or we can ignore that Spirit, climb off the cross, and do our own thing. Paul hopes we will choose the former.

Galatians 6:14 summarizes Paul's desire for our relationships, and for our entire lives: "May I never boast except in the cross of our Lord Jesus Christ, through which the world has been crucified to me, and I to the world." For any Christian, that's the standard. We are crucified to the world. All the shame and pain of the cross is to be a daily experience for us. Both in our relationship with Christ, and in our relationships with others, the cross symbolizes the depth to which we are called to kill self.

That death, however, is not a means of gaining God's favor. It is a response to the fact that we already have that favor. John Stott puts it well, ". . . one might say, every Christian is both a Simon of Cyrene and a Barabbas. Like Barabbas we escape the cross, for Christ died in our place. Like Simon of Cyrene we carry the cross, for he calls us to take it up and follow him."[11]

Because you've escaped the cross, pick it up. Pick it up for your spouse. Pick it up for your children. Pick it up for your friend. Pick it up for that stranger. Pick it up and die, so that those relationships can live.

Endnotes

1. Dr. Ralph Underwager, *Voices* (November 12, 1993).

2. "ἀφορμή," Walter Bauer, *A Greek-English Lexicon of the New Testament and Other Early Christian Literature*, translated by William F. Arndt and F. Wilbur Gingrich (Chicago: University of Chicago Press, 1979), 127.

3. "ἔχθρα," Bauer 331.

4. "ἔρις," Bauer 309.

5. "ζῆλος," Bauer 337-338.

6. "θυμός," Bauer 365.

7. "ἐριθεία," Bauer 309.

8. "διχοστασία," Bauer 200; "αἵρεσις," Bauer 23-24.

9. "φθόνος," Bauer 359.

10. Shelton, *As the Romans Did* (New York: Oxford University Press, 1988), 277-287, quoting Cicero, *The Prosecution of Verres*.

11. John Stott, *The Cross of Christ* (Downers Grove, IL: Inter-Varsity Press, 1986), 279.

Study Questions

1. The chapter begins by listing two common misconceptions about Christianity. Some wrongly believe that God's will is for us to have no conditions — we get to do what we want. Others wrongly believe that God's will is for us to have no freedom — we must earn our way to heaven. Which misconception do you struggle with the most? Explain how each misconception would affect day to day relationships between people.

2. Paul lists at least eight diseases which result when we misunderstand grace. Which disease do you struggle with the most in your own relationships? In what ways is that struggle tied to a possible misunderstanding of the cross?

3. What specific relationship has suffered in your life by your refusal to climb on a cross and die? What do you need to do to mend that relationship?

4. How can we be both free from law and slaves to serving and loving?

5. Why won't a good dose of law (do's and do not's) fully resolve relationship issues?

6. How would your relationships in the following areas change if you climbed on a cross daily in each of them: at home, at work, at play?

7. Share someone in your life who exemplifies what it means to be crucified in relationships.

8. Which fruit of the Spirit is needed most in your relationships?

9. How do we allow the Spirit to help us die, to bear better fruit, and to bring healing into our relationships?

Part Four

Part Four

Reflections on the Cross

It's one thing to dive into a mountain pool and explore the trout swimming its currents and the pebbles decorating its bottom. It's another to survey the pool from a distance, noting the cluster of aspens nearby and the backdrop of mountains scraping the sky. In the first three parts of this book, we dove deeply into the pool of the cross. We explored its secrets to a disturbing depth. In this last section of the book, we'll resurface, dry off, hike a mile away, and turn around to survey the cross at a distance. We'll note how it blends into and contrasts with its surroundings. We'll note how it blends into and contrasts with our lives.

If you haven't already, take off your shoes and find a comfortable spot. This section isn't for digging and cataloging as much as it is for reflecting and meditating. Now is the time to apply the cross to your life. Now is the time to come face to face not only with the cross, but with the man on the cross. Now is the time to ask what all this means for you.

Turn off the TV, say goodnight to the kids and spend some time reflecting on the cross.

† 8 †

Of Kings and Crosses

Thursday afternoon I met a king.

Up to that point, it had been just another Thursday. The sun glowed warmly. The wind gently whispered. And the traffic hummed a steady rhythm as I pedaled a mountain bike to my office at the Christian Student Center. Little did I know that on that afternoon, I would meet a king.

But as I stepped into the Student Center, someone grabbed my hand and led me to a short, curly-haired man surrounded by a clan of college students. I found myself face to face with a king. King Mongo they called him.

Unfortunately, my surprise faded to skepticism as I talked with Mongo. I don't think it was the gold ring on his small toe, or the new t-shirt with his name on it, or even his multicolored car parked outside which fed my doubts. It wasn't the oddity of this king which troubled me. It was his lack of credentials. They weren't quite what I expected.

The Cross: Saved by the Shame of It All

According to King Mongo, he had run for the office of mayor in Memphis every year for the past thirteen years — and had lost just as many times. Since it was obvious that his title of "king" had not been earned by superhuman achievements, I silently questioned the source of his kingship. Yet despite his failure, I was intrigued. So I continued to listen. And my patience paid off. I soon learned the origin of Mongo's title.

His crown did not come from Memphis. It didn't come from Tennessee. It didn't come from the United States. In fact, it wasn't even granted by anyone on the planet. The source of his crown was a little known planet in an even less known galaxy. King Mongo claimed to be a ruler from the planet Zambodia and was on a mission to save the city of Memphis from crooked councilmen and pompous politicians.

While some people claimed he was crazy and rumored that he had once visited an institution, his intelligence and wit betrayed as sane a man as any I met that day. He was no lunatic. He was simply a carefree man doing what men have done through the ages. He wanted to wear a crown without the conquests. He wanted the title without the trials. Mongo just wanted to be king for a day. And it didn't matter what kind of story he had to weave in order to wear that crown.

Mongo's well-meaning but credential-lacking royalty is certainly one way to gain a crown. Simply claim the title of king despite all the facts and despite all pictures of reality. That well-worn path has been traveled by many in the past. It hasn't, however, produced much in the way of quality kings. And few are the people who actually believe such a claim.

It seems to have been this issue which veiled the eyes of the ones who stood with the Messiah on his last day. Those in the crowd that Friday thought Jesus was as crazy as King Mongo. They didn't believe his claim of kingship any more than they believed in space shuttles or televisions. As far as they were concerned, Jesus did not possess the qualifications of a king. He had no credentials.

So instead of honoring him, they hit him. Instead of worshiping him, they waged war against him. Instead of exaltation, they delivered execution. All references to the kingship of Jesus in his final hours were simply taunts:

The soldiers beat Jesus, threw a purple robe on his back, and teased, "Hail, king of the Jews!" (John 19:3).

The Jews forced Pilate's hand by persuading him of the harmful (but imaginary) implications of this self-proclaimed king from Galilee: "If you let this man go, you are no friend of Caesar. Anyone who claims to be a king opposes Caesar" (John 19:12).

The Chief priests diagnosed Jesus' claims as crazy when they proclaimed, "We have no king but Caesar" (John 19:15).

Yet among all the references to the kingship of Jesus that last day, none are more telling than those found at the foot of the cross. For the crowd gathered at the bottom of the death stake did not merely taunt the Galilean, they demanded proof of his claim. They too understood that the crown of royalty could not be worn by just anyone. It must be earned. It must be proven.

Two specific remarks floated in the air that afternoon which show the evidence the crowd demanded:

The Cross: Saved by the Shame of It All

"He's the King of Israel! Let him come down now from the cross, and we will believe in him" (Matt 27:42, author's paraphrase).

"If you are the King of the Jews, save yourself" (Luke 23:37).

In the eyes of the crowd at Golgotha, the only way for Jesus to prove his kingship was to come *down* from the cross. It was the cross which marred his résumé. It was the cross which negated his credentials. If he would save *himself*, then they would believe. Kings don't hang on crosses, they thought. Kings don't lie helplessly anchored onto two timbers by three spikes.

But Jesus painted a different picture of king that day. The proof of his royalty was not to be found in his absence from the cross. It was to be found in his very presence *on* the cross. The crowd said a true king would come down. Jesus said only a true king would remain. The crowd clamored that the proof of his claim rested in his ability to leave the cross. Jesus said the proof was in his ability to cling to the cross. And while the crowd taunted him to save himself, Jesus instead chose to save — us.

Such is the picture of the cross. For some it was merely the death of a power-hungry, reality-blurred usurper of the throne. But for us, it was the death of the true King for his subjects. It was the sacrifice of the Creator for his creation. It was the life of a Son, for the lives of sinners.

Jesus. He wasn't quite the king they expected. But he is more a king than we could ever dream.

Study Questions

1. King Mongo wanted the crown without the cross. In what ways is that true for us when it comes to Christianity? Is there a specific area of your life where you have tried to gain glory without sacrifice?

2. What is it about the cross which made it so difficult for people to accept that a king could be on one? Would you have accepted Jesus' claim of kingship if you had been there that Friday and witnessed his crucifixion?

3. How does Jesus' presence on the cross change your view of what it means to be a king?

4. Why didn't Jesus come off the cross, even momentarily, to prove to his doubters that he truly was who he said he was?

5. Explain how Jesus' presence on the cross gives him the fullest credentials possible to be both your Savior from sins and the Lord of your life.

✦ 9 ✦

The Great Exchange

Juicy chunks of tomatoes.

Soft brown beans.

Spicy ground beef swimming in an even spicier sauce.

It was my mom's homemade chili. And as a seven year old with a sweet tooth, I hated it. In fact hate was a soft word compared to what my stomach told me when I lifted the spoon to my mouth. But I wasn't alone. My twin brother Craig also hated it. We disliked it so much that we devised a perfect plan to satisfy both our stomachs and our parents.

There was a standing rule in our house that if you took over 45 minutes to eat, you were sent to your room to finish dinner alone. Thus every time we had chili, Craig and I ate a little slower, and talked a little more. We were just waiting for that clock to signal the time for our escape. And when 45 minutes had passed, Mom repeated the rule and sent us with steaming bowls and smiling faces to our rooms.

The Cross: Saved by the Shame of It All

Among the many items in our room was a large pine toy box. It was painted with blue cartoon figures and filled with all our toys. It was our favorite item — not only because of what it contained, but also because of how it could be used. Upon entering our room, Craig and I would scamper to the toy box on the far side of the room. With a little effort, we pulled the pine box away from the wall and dumped the chili, bean by ugly bean, behind the toy box. Once the deed was done, we pushed the box as far up against the wall as we could. And two hungry but happy boys played until we thought enough time had passed. Then we marched out and presented two empty chili bowls to our Mom.

And so it went week after week, month after month. Mom was happier and the chili pile behind the toy box got higher and harder. It was the perfect plan — except for one thing: seven-year-old boys don't realize how bad multi-month-old chili can smell. But parents do. And they did.

As Dad stood towering above us that day he discovered the chili pile, the call for confession came: "Who did this? Who is responsible for this?" In the seconds it took for Dad to ask his question, my small mind raced and determined that the truth better be told. I would speak. I would reveal who had committed such an atrocity.

"Craig did it!" I pointed my finger, Dad turned his eyes, and Craig's mouth dropped open. Before another word could be spoken, punishment was meted out with the palm of a hand on the rear and a command to remain in the room until further notice. Craig lay weeping in bed and I slowly walked off guilty, but free. Unknowingly and unwillingly, Craig had performed the greatest act of service one can provide — he took the punishment of a guilty person.

Things like that don't happen very often. When they happen on a grander scale, they make headlines. They become the frontliner in the news programs or are made into prime time television movies.

It's a rare thing for someone to exchange places with the guilty. But it's an even rarer thing when the one who takes the blame has the earthen clay from which he formed man under his fingernails, and the breath of man's life stirring in his breast.

The last week of Jesus' life carries some of the harshest ironies and most perplexing injustices the Galilean ever faced. Multitudes of "sinners" welcomed him to Jerusalem while circles of "saints" frowned in the background. Thirty silver coins tempted one of the twelve men closest to Jesus to sell his Lord and his soul. A jury and judge of top religious leaders found Jesus guilty on multiple counts while the city and county judges found no basis for any charges. Twelve men who had left all to follow Jesus finally even left Jesus. And the same crowd that welcomed Jesus to Jerusalem also sent him to the cross.

The very ones whom Jesus had come to release now bound him and threw him into prison. He was rushed through a makeshift trial where the jury was either half asleep or well paid. The key witnesses spoke of events they never witnessed. By the flickering light of candles in the early morning mist, a judge and jury of no integrity passed down a sentence of no hope: death to the Messiah.

But perhaps the oddest and most startling scene is found in Luke's peculiar description of the series of events after the trial. Jesus is sent to Pilate, then to Herod, then back to Pilate, whose fear of the crowd is greater than his understanding of the truth. In the heat of the moment Pilate can no longer withstand the pull of the crowd, and he yields to their shouts. Luke records the next step in Luke 23:25: "He released the man who had been thrown into prison for insurrection and murder . . . and surrendered Jesus to their will."

Did your eyes catch the heart-stopping reversal in that single act? One man is given freedom, the other receives condemnation. An exchange of sentences. Death is given life. Life is given death.

This is no ordinary exchange. It's not like the movie where an innocent man is mistakenly thrown into jail only later to be released when the true criminal is found. Here, it's not the gate of the innocent man that swings open. It's the cell door of the guilty man that swings open. As he exits, an innocent man enters. The murderer walks out. The Master walks in.

One was a man who had scarred others. He had taken life. He had caused trouble. He was violent. The other was a man who had touched others. He had given life. He was a peacemaker. He was compassionate.

But this is not just a story of one fortunate criminal. This exchange between a Scarface and a Savior freed not only Barabbas, but us. For as the six inch Roman nails were forced into the skin and bone of a peaceful Messiah, they didn't merely penetrate flesh and wood. They reached deeper. Much deeper. With each blow of the Roman soldier's hammer, those spikes pierced the rusted locks on our cells of sin, fear, and confusion. And as the stone exploded from the tomb three days later, so did cell doors across the lives of humanity.

The cell of sin which had been ours became his. Sentences of death and pardon were exchanged. The noose by which we were to hang fell upon him. The shining blade of the guillotine was stopped short of our necks by the neck of Jesus.

Yet unlike those he had freed, this voluntary convict named Jesus had the power to unlock his own cell. No door would hold him, no guard could restrain him. And as the first ray of freedom hit our faces, it was the hand of Jesus that led us out of the rubble into the plains. It was his touch that cleared the dust from our eyes. And it was his warmth which dispelled the shadows.

There has never been a greater exchange.

Study Questions

1. Share a time when someone took the blame for you. Did they do it voluntarily or because they had no other choice?

2. What if Jesus had been forced to take our place on the cross instead of doing it voluntarily? Would that change your appreciation for the cross?

3. Describe how Barabbas must have felt when he walked free and Jesus stood condemned.

4. How would your life change if you lived every day knowing that a "great exchange" had taken place in your life?

5. What are some ways today that we can exchange ourselves for others?

10

Gardens

I.

"In this battle, death will not be one path among many — it will be the only path."

The recent words of his Father pierced the Prince's heart and rang in his head like a steel hammer. They seemed so harsh and unreal in contrast to the peace and beauty of the garden through which he now strolled. Clothed in a brilliant white robe, he thoughtfully stepped along the garden pathway that danced through a collage of soft blue flowers intermixed with gentle pink ones. Just within his hearing, though out of sight, a stream bubbled happily through the adjacent golden meadow.

Timeless hands caressed a white flower which swayed elegantly in a breeze. He remembered the times past when he and his Father the King had walked together along the same path. Now alone, he reflected on the recent conversation with his Father in the throne room. The King told him that plans were being made, and their creative forces would be combined to give birth to a new world. He shook with excitement as he thought of the possibilities.

It was not easy to comprehend such plans, however, and it had taken his breath away when he heard his Father continue. Their forces would also be combined to create new living creatures. Man and Woman they would be called. Already he had fallen in love with them, though they were still a mere thought. While he was excited, he was also quite anxious, for the King had told him of another plan that would have to be put into effect with the birth of the new creatures — a battle plan.

His mind was brimming with these thoughts as he moved toward the stream, crossed a sea of golden stalks in the meadow, and rested by the water's edge. The water raced by him, begging to take his troubled thoughts from him. Glowing light, emanating from the castle in the distance, brought a familiar feeling of security. He closed his eyes and thought, his spirit filling with an explosive mixture of joy and anxiety.

Already he could hear the clash of swords as a powerful struggle between his kingdom and another's would ensue for the creation and creatures soon to come.

"Death will not be one path among many . . . ."

The words rang through the halls of his soul.

II.

As the Prince watched from above, small tremors shook the ground, the thundering power of the creative forces diminishing as the creation drew to completion. Delicate sheets of steam crawled from the moist ground into the air, and the Prince watched his and his Father's work consummate. He felt joy in seeing this creation take form and in seeing its new inhabitants take the first steps in a virgin land.

Through the clouds, he intently watched as Man, then Woman, awoke in the sunlit garden which crowned the creation. The perfect place for such lovely ones, he thought. He leaned back, allowing a divine silence to fall upon the garden. His Father placed an arm around him as they both lovingly gazed at their new children.

He observed the children as they lifted their eyes towards the sky, meeting his. His heart beat faster as he met their gaze. All of the effort and planning had been worth it. He couldn't remember a time when he had felt so full of love and happiness. For several moments the Prince and the children stood locked in a loving stare.

Soon, however, he was aware of another presence, one not in his line of vision, and he turned for a closer look. As he averted his eyes, so did Man and Woman. There was someone else in the garden, one whom the Prince knew too well, and one whom he wished had not come. Grief and frustration filled his eyes as he watched the arrogant king of another kingdom saunter into the garden. From his lofty vantage point, the Prince silently watched a terrifying scene unfold.

The king, smelling of sulphur and smoke, his body dripping stenching liquid, confidently strode into the garden. Man and Woman were noticeably frightened by the king's presence and backed several steps away. As quickly as they caught sight of him they lost him, for the shape of the king was soon hidden in a shining glow which began to grow in front of him. The closer the king came, the brighter the glow became. Soon they saw nothing except the strange and seductive glow which hid the king from their sight. The glow seemed to almost hypnotize Man and Woman, and they were unable to unfix their stare from it. It moved ever closer to them and finally stopped a few feet in front of them. Man and Woman searched the glow to find its source. They finally noticed a small box which floated in the center of the light. Dark jewels decorated its edges and delicate carvings wound through its golden surface.

"You may have it and all its wondrous contents if you wish," the evil king said from behind the glow, still hidden.

"What does it contain?" questioned Woman.

Almost whispering, barely audible to the Prince, the evil king, the Deceiver, pronounced, "Only that which you most desire. Take it, and you will be happy. It will fill your soul with true joy. Take it and enjoy its riches."

The Prince stared as Man and Woman hesitantly reached for the small promising box, silently pleading with them not to take it.

"Oh yes," the Deceiver added quickly, "should you take the box and enjoy its pleasures, I must ask that you leave your King and your Prince, and join my kingdom. In view of what the box contains, however, it is a small price to pay."

A second of eternity passed, and as the Prince watched, Man and Woman reached through the brilliant glow for the box, hastily grabbed it, and lifted its lid. The small lid flew effortlessly open to reveal — nothing! The strange and captivating glow vanished, and the warm light that had filled the garden fled. It was replaced by a peculiar chill. Man and Woman stood face to face with the hideous king, the glow no longer hiding him. They raised their hands to the Prince, begging for help. As they lifted their hands, two silver rings appeared, one on Man's hand and one on Woman's hand.

"A little token to remember your decision here today. They will never come off, and they will always symbolize your covenant with me," the evil king sneered.

The Prince, tears clinging to his sullen face, knew that nothing of real value had filled the box. Yet the deed was done.

"Leave the garden," boomed the voice of the Father towards Man and Woman. "You have made your decision, and you must leave."

"You must go," cried the shaking voice of the Prince. "You cannot stay here any longer. You must go."

Then the Prince bent down with his Father and heard his Father as he whispered quietly to Man and Woman, "But you will not be alone."

Man and Woman looked at the Prince, their hands, and then the ground. Slowly, they walked away, following their new king. The Prince watched until they were out of sight.

The Prince could do nothing. They had made their choice, and they were the first casualties of war. He knew that by this one act, the Deceiver had declared war. Behind him he could hear the armies of the kingdom gathering. Fading echoes of the battle trumpet passed over his ears, bringing a slight chill to his skin.

His Father's voice brought him back to reality. "The battle has begun, just as we knew it would."

"I wish with all of my heart that it didn't have to. But I know that we could not escape it. We must get them back. We must free them."

The Prince felt his Father's massive hand on his shoulder. "Son, can you do it?"

"Yes, I can, and I will." Yet he knew that what lay ahead would test every strand of his being.

The Prince turned from the earthly garden, and strode towards the castle to prepare himself for battle.

III.

The warm fluid environment left him as the Prince was forcefully pushed by his mother's contractions into the cold air. The comfort and hypnotic rhythm of his mother's heartbeat was replaced by the frightened calls of sheep and goats in the small stable. His feeble body shook uncontrollably, protesting the airy and chilly environment. His head ached with a dull pain and his lungs burned as they tried to work.

He felt himself lifted high by a strange grip below his neck, and his tiny hands waved in front of his eyes. The Prince struggled to move his head to view the new surroundings, but his weak muscles disobeyed and only allowed his head to flop from side to side. A feeling of helplessness began to rise within him as he felt the constraints of his new infant limbs.

Suddenly his entire body was enveloped, not by the

warmth and safety of the womb, but by a soft cloth. It brought its own unique comfort to him. Then he felt himself being lowered to the ground and gently placed on the tan straw. Fuzzy grey objects filled his eyes and he realized that he was seeing his father the carpenter for the first time through the eyes of a newborn. One grey form left and another slightly different appeared. Then he heard the consoling voice of his mother who so often had sung to him while he was still forming.

He had not been prepared for this experience, and he struggled to realize that his mighty form had been reduced to the body of an infant. Yet he knew it had to be done. The first step in the battle plan was complete. He had successfully infiltrated the battleground. The Creator had taken the form of the creation. Soon he would face the Deceiver, not in the majesty and splendor of his previous form, but in the frail and finite body of the creation.

Do they know? Do these two have any idea of what is to come? Will they understand? Questions silently filled the Prince's mind.

A tiredness washed over him and he had to stop his frantic thoughts. He was exhausted from the long hours of labor, and he needed to rest. Miniature eyelids closed as the Prince fell asleep.

Rest . . . I must rest. There will be much to do soon.

IV.

"Teacher! . . . Teacher!!"

The words broke the early morning stillness in Jerusalem as they reached the Prince's ears. They were tinged with the sarcasm that he had come to hear so often since his birth into the world thirty years ago. He wanted to ignore them, and continue talking to the crowd that had gathered. He wanted to speak about the Father and his love for them. But he knew he must listen. For he knew that with the words came a test — a test from the Deceiver.

The Prince kept his head turned towards the crowd, but he could hear them coming. Agents of the Deceiver rode on sandled feet towards him. They were joined by the piercing shriek of a woman who was being dragged with them. The sandals stopped behind him, as did the woman's shriek.

"Teacher!"

The Prince slowly turned his head away from the crowd and towards the one who had called him. A dark-skinned man wore a black cloak and a sword-filled scabbard at his side. The Prince gazed down to the man's right hand and saw a large jeweled ring on his obese finger. Judging by the size of the ring and the evil grin upon his face, he must have taken the box long ago. He was surrounded by a small troop which stared coldly at the Prince with dead eyes.

Poor man, can't he see the deception? the Prince thought.

Slowly the Prince's eyes left the dark man and found the woman who was the source of the shriek. She wore only a small blanket which she clutched with white knuckles, trying to cover herself. The man's hand was firmly placed on her neck. The woman's eyes were downcast, looking up only in quick glances.

After a moment, she lifted her tearstained face and met the Prince's gaze. Her expression revealed fear and her eyes spoke deeply of shame. The Prince saw the small silver band on her right hand. It spoke even more clearly of her deed.

She too had taken the box. She too had grasped it. Another casualty, the Prince thought.

The dark man spoke up. "Teacher, we caught this woman opening the box. According to your law, she should be put to death." He let out a small chuckle. "What do you think we should do with her?"

Tested again!? Why? Why can't they see? The Prince agonized as he realized that the very creation he had strived to make was now turning on him, trying to trap him.

His face grew warmer as his heart beat faster. Opening his mouth slightly, he drew in a deep breath to calm himself.

I could wipe out this entire troop with one swipe of my sword, he thought. His fingers felt the smooth handle of the sword strapped at his side, then quickly dropped and relaxed.

"Those who open the box must die. This woman has opened the box, therefore, she deserves to die."

At the Prince's comment, the troops cheered.

"And you may kill her . . . on one condition. Let the man whose fingers have never opened the box be the first to strike her."

The troop's cheers quickly lost volume, and silence again filled the air. The Prince glanced at the man and his ragged troops, waiting to see their move. Then, after a few moments, the men left, one by one. They slowly walked away down the dusty path that weaved in between the buildings of the city. Even the crowd that the Prince had been talking to dispersed, and the Prince stood alone with the woman. He lifted his hand and placed it under her chin.

"It's all right. They have gone. Everything is fine."

"Thank you. Thank you so much. But what about this?"

She raised her hand to reveal the small ring which was on it. As she raised it, tears began to fall from her eyes.

"I can help you."

The Prince stepped back and quickly drew his sword. The woman, her hand still raised, looked at the Prince in horror. As the Prince raised his sword above his head, the woman cried loudly in fear. The Prince swung the sword downward with all of his strength. The sharp blade met the ring on the woman's hand and sheared through it, stopping short of the woman's flesh. Two silver half circles flew through the air, landing a few feet away. The woman looked down at her hand, amazed at what she saw.

"You are free now. He has no more power over you. You are free to follow the one who loves you."

The Prince turned and walked away, leaving the amazed woman. Other battles and tests awaited him.

V.

His breathing was labored and came in heavy gasps as his body racked with weariness. Falling to his knees beneath a low hanging tree, the Prince rested. Weary eyes gazed through the darkness searching for the Deceiver. The Prince's hands shook from the anticipation he felt inside. Fifteen years ago they had been the skillful and graceful hands of a carpenter. Now they bled and were scarred with the callouses of battle.

His body leaned against a rock, begging him to quit. The Deceiver, upon seeing the Prince's arrival tonight, had disappeared into the foliage which filled the hillside garden overlooking Jerusalem. Sitting there, the Prince's mind flooded with thoughts about the past years of fighting. So many people had trusted the empty promise of the Deceiver that the Prince's task was almost too much. As he thought about it, he became angry, breathing heavier and harder all the while.

Through many towns and villages he had fought, cutting the covenant rings of those who had been led into the evil kingdom. Most of the fighting had been brief, and usually with agents of the Deceiver, never the Deceiver himself. Tonight, however, he knew he would face the Deceiver. Finally, a meeting between the two was to take place. A meeting that would decide the war once and for all.

It was ironic, he thought, that the war for this world and its people which had begun so long ago in a garden, should end in a garden. The battle plans made long ago had sounded so good, so powerful. Yet now, with his body aching and his mind spinning, they had become less appealing. The other fights had been nothing. They only prepared him for tonight. This night was what the whole battle pointed to. Nothing else mattered.

Yet he came reluctantly tonight. For tonight he knew that he had not been called to fight, but merely to submit. Tonight there would be a death. He knew that the plans did not call for the death of the Deceiver, but his own.

As he sat with his thoughts, he was filled with hatred for the Deceiver and what he had done, and with fear for what lay ahead. He remembered how the Deceiver's box had been offered to him in the past and how he had resisted it. Yet tonight the Deceiver's box had begun to look much more appealing. Tonight the box offered a chance to go back home, a chance to escape death. The Prince knew that if he took it, he could return to his home in Nazareth. The fighting would be over, and he could rest again.

He longed for the crisp mornings when he would wake to hear his mother's singing in the next room while she prepared breakfast. He had little strength left to defend himself, much less to do what the plans called for. All he had to do to be free of this and to avoid death was to take the ornamented box.

The full moon created dancing shadows throughout the garden. Below, the sounds of the city of Jerusalem could be heard, the people oblivious of the fight about to be fought above them.

Yes, he thought, it would be nice to go home.

Suddenly, without warning, the flash of a sword full of the moon's light darted in front of his eyes. His arm reeled with pain. The sword sunk deep into his flesh. As the Prince turned towards the owner of the sword, his eyes met those of the Deceiver — fiery red dots against the blackness of the night. In a rage, he quickly drew his sword, and gathered himself onto his feet.

I do not want to die! I do not! The desperate cries raced through his mind as energy surged through his body and he engaged the enemy.

The swords crashed and snapped together, metal cutting metal, sparks flying from the force of the blows. The Prince fought with frustration and desperation.

For the first few moments, the fight was a stalemate. The Prince's sword found its way into the Deceiver's flesh, digging deep. And with equal persistence, the Deceiver's sword contacted the Prince's flesh.

After several moments of fighting, however, the battle began to tip in the Prince's favor. His sword became more accurate, and his desperation greater. Standing toe to toe with his opponent, he fought for his life. As his sword cut and slashed, moving almost automatically, the voices of home and fatigue called him. He realized that with his position, he could inflict one serious injury, turn, and walk away. It would be as easy as that. One hard thrust, and he could walk away free. He would not have to die. He could end it here.

Yet as quickly as that thought entered his mind, it was countered by another. He was reminded of the mission for which he had come to the garden tonight, a costly one. He knew that if he stayed in the garden, and allowed himself to take a solid blow from the Deceiver, the plan would be accomplished. One blow with all of the Deceiver's power and fury unleashed behind it would free the rest of creation. He could bear the consequence of every hand that had lifted the lid of the box, and free them at the same time. Yet the blow would be instantly fatal.

The fear of dying and the need to fulfill the plans became two opposing thoughts which fought inside his mind, each vying for victory. As the struggle continued within him, and the battle without grew, it became almost unbearable. The sounds of war crescendoed to an overwhelming intensity.

Finally one thought gained the victory, and the Prince stopped. He withdrew his sword from the battle, stepped back three steps, and stopped. The Deceiver, on the ground before him, rose, disbelief showing in his eyes. He moved toward the Prince until he was inches from him. The Prince could feel the hot and sulphurous breath of the Deceiver on his leathery face. A wicked smile flashed across the Deceiver's face, and the Prince, seconds ago burning hot from physical effort, now shivered in the still of the night air. Silence enveloped the two, broken only by the sounds of weighted breathing. The Prince's feet screamed to run and his arm screamed to raise his sword, yet he remained still, holding his sword tightly to his side.

Stepping back again, the Prince allowed space to come between himself and the enemy. Calling every ounce of strength left, he commanded his hand to release his sword. His hand protested, but then obeyed, and the sword fell to the ground with a thud. The Prince breathed deeply, slowly raised his head, and looked at his enemy.

His eyes were met with a sarcastic and heinous laugh from the Deceiver. As the Prince watched, the

Deceiver cautiously raised his two handed double-edged sword above his head. The razor-like edges glistened in the moonlight. A loud, guttural cry emerged from the Deceiver's throat, and his muscles flexed in readiness.

The Prince, now more confident, closed his eyes. As his eyelids hit the bottom, he heard the silent whisper of the Deceiver's sword as it left its upright position, and swung through the air. He knew that it would find its target with deadly accuracy. Darkness fell.

VI.

Shaking legs carried a spent soldier. They carried him through the familiar garden, though his eyes were oblivious to its beauty. Instead his eyes focussed on a humped figure that was sitting near the stream. He walked quicker now, passing through the golden meadow and drawing nearer to the figure. Almost running now, the soldier finally reached the figure, and stood before it. The soldier recognized the figure to be that of the King. The King raised his head, revealing eyes which dripped with tears. But as they met the glance of the soldier, they immediately opened with happiness.

The Prince threw his arms around the King's neck, hugging with all of his might. "They are free. I'm home Father, I'm home."

Study Questions

1. God and Jesus knew the disgraceful nature of the cross, yet planned to use it to accomplish their plan even before our creation (1 Pet 1:18-21). Why? What other methods of death could they have chosen, and why did they reject those in favor of the cross?

2. In terms of his earthly life, what sort of things would Jesus have been tempted to embrace in order to escape the cross?

3. Explain how the cross truly is the climax of a battle which started in the Garden of Eden.

4. In what ways does it help you to know that Jesus struggled as he thought about embracing death (see Luke 22:39-46)? In what sense was the battle actually won there in that garden?

5. The story presents sin as a covenant agreement — when we sin we enter into covenant with the Enemy. Explain how that is true. How does the cross eliminate the covenant of sin?

✳11✳

Good-byes*

"Well Dad, I guess we're going to go."

I heard the words leave my lips, yet it was hard to believe I was saying them. My wife and I were visiting my dad and stepmom in my hometown of Cloudcroft, New Mexico. It would be the last time before we moved to Memphis. Both of us were excited about the thought of moving, yet it was strange saying good-bye. I had never really said good-bye to someone like this before.

In the waning light of dusk, I turned and hugged my stepmom as we stood in the dining room where I had eaten so many meals. She held me close for a minute, then let go and hugged my wife Kendra.

"Gee, this isn't too bad," I pondered. I imagined it was going to be harder.

I looked at my stepmom after she released Kendra,

---

*"Good-byes" first appeared as "A Son Says Goodbye" in *Image* magazine 7 (Jan/Feb 1991).

and tears began to flow from her eyes. She grabbed me hard and we hugged again.

"I didn't plan on crying."

"That's OK," I said, "I don't have that many people who cry over me."

We hugged for awhile, then I turned to my dad.

My dad.

The one I used to hang on to for dear life as we went flying through the woods on his motorcycle. The one who used to race my brother and me down the icy ski slopes on weekends. The one who gave so that we would have. We hugged each other tightly.

"I love you."

"I love you too, Dad."

As I hugged him with my face buried in his chest, I thought to myself, "This still isn't too bad. My eyes are still dry. My heart is still beating. I'll see them again. This isn't good-bye forever."

I let go of my dad and looked into his face. As we stood silently gazing at each other, our eyes said what our mouths couldn't find the words to say.

"Take care of yourself."

All the time this was happening, I kept thinking to myself, "This good-bye stuff isn't that bad. It's easier than I thought."

I looked up at my dad again, ready to walk to the entry way, and out the door.

Then I took a step.

Whoom! A red hot knife thrust itself into my heart, and my breath left for a moment.

I was leaving! (It was finally beginning to sink in.)

This would be last time for a long time that I would step though this entryway. This was the last time for awhile that I would be face to face with my dad.

I looked at Dad again. A rare tear had found its way into the corner of his eye.

I took another step.

Whoom! Another knife found a home in my heart.

We passed through the entryway with its antique table and aged pictures to the red tile porch outside. The cool mountain air felt good, because I had suddenly began to sweat. We stopped for one last moment together and hugged.

More daggers.

Now I just wanted to get out of there. I was hurting, really hurting, and I could feel tears rising up quickly. I said a final "good-bye" and walked up the decaying cement sidewalk to our car. As I reached the car, I turned and waved.

"This is hard!" I thought.

We got into the car, put it in gear, and drove off. I honked twice, very weakly, and watched my dad disappear in the rearview mirror.

"Are you OK?" my wife asked.

I turned to her, forced a smile that we both knew was fake, and said nothing.

As we drove away, tears began to fall and a son felt the burden of saying good-bye to his father.

Almost two thousand years ago a very similar, but more serious scene took place.

The majestic circle of angels and heavenly beings who normally resounded with shouts of glory around the throne of God was now ominously silent. The royal halls that had sounded with praise for all eternity, became silent for the first time. All eyes were cast downward as a Father shared a precious moment with His Son.

"Father, it's time. I must go."

Red hot daggers cut through both hearts.

"Yes, I know Son. The time is right."

The Son stepped away from the throne and took a last loving look at the Father. Twin tears fell, one from the eye of the Son and the other from the eye of the Father. Their eyes locked for a few more moments, each longing to make the scene last, each knowing that good-bye must be said.

The Son took one more step back, turned, and left.

And that which had been eternally united — separated.

That which had been One from the beginning — was now Two.

And the word which had never been heard in all the celestial halls now resounded like a death bell: "Good-bye."

A Father said good-bye to a Son.

Unity was painfully separated by love, for our sake. How wonderful to have a Father who understands the burden of saying good-bye. And better yet, how wonderful to have a Father who experienced the deepest pain of all by saying good-bye to his only Son, so that he could say welcome to you and me.

Study Questions

1. Share a time when you experienced a tearful good-bye.

2. Read John 1:1-18. Explain the differences between our good-byes and the good-bye experienced by God and Jesus when the Word, who was God, became flesh.

3. In what ways did the inevitability of the cross make that initial good-bye even worse?

4. Explain the difference between the separation of God and Jesus as Jesus came to earth, and the separation of God and Jesus as Jesus became sin on the cross (Mark 15:33-34; 1 Peter 2:23-24; 2 Cor 5:21).

5. In what ways is the cross our "good-bye" to sinful desires and actions? Why do we have such a difficult time making that good-bye permanent?

+12+

Take the Hand

It was so faint, we barely heard it. But as I stuck the key into the doorknob of our apartment, a breeze carried the sound to our ears — the thin cry of a scared kitten. We stepped down the walkway towards the yard and saw her. There, just at the edge of the warm glow of one of the yard lights, a black kitten shivered in the cold crying for help. Maybe she had lost her way. Maybe she was hurt. But now, in desperation, she had come to the one place that might offer some hope.

I carefully walked backwards, went into the apartment, and poured a bowl of milk while Kendra tried to walk closer to the kitten. But when I returned, I saw a frustrating scene. Every time Kendra inched closer to the kitten, the kitten retreated a few steps. Yet she still cried for help. I walked towards her and held out my hand with the bowl of milk, hoping that she would understand. But she only retreated more, all the while crying desperate pleas for warmth, acceptance, and nourishment. It was a terrible feeling.

We moved still closer, calling softly and holding out the bowl of milk, but finally she turned and ran. The uncertainty of the situation was too much for her, so she ran back into the darkness which had caused her pains and had sent her to the light in the first place.

We had all the kitten needed, all she could have hoped for. Yet in her desperation, her hesitancy overcame her hope — and she ran.

Perhaps she had too many encounters with the wrong type of people.

Perhaps she had learned early not to trust people.

Perhaps the desperation of the situation clouded her judgment.

She had come with hope. Yet just at the moment her hope could be realized, she ran.

Jessica's voice on the phone shook with uncertainty.

"I just don't know. I'm scared to really look into it. I'm scared about what I might find."

I had met Jessica two weeks ago and had called her to see how she was. I found myself encouraging a skeptical and scared college freshman to take a look at Christianity.

"What if I find out that it's too boring? I don't want to be bored for the rest of my life."

She was in unfamiliar territory.

"And as long as I don't look at it, I won't have to change. I'm afraid that if I look, I'll see that I'll have to change, then I won't want to change, but then I'll feel guilty for not changing . . . ."

Her voice raised in intensity. She had been raised by a mother who espoused reincarnation. She had been educated by a group of friends whose only knowledge of God was what they read in the newspapers and heard on the radio.

"I'm just not happy. I don't know what I want. I've been thinking about packing up and leaving. I think maybe I will find what I need somewhere else, and if I don't, I'll just keep moving. I have a friend in Spain who said I could go down there . . . ."

Hurting. Confused. Scared. The dissatisfaction of life pushed her to face a God she didn't know. She realized that her life was not what it was meant to be. But her view of God was not what it was meant to be either. Worldly preachers, confused parents, and sin-sick friends had made her think of God more as a foe than a friend, and the life of a Christian more as a life of boredom than of fulfillment.

She had come to the point in life where she finally realized she needed more. But she was scared. Too scared to see that behind the screen of false images stood a God with outstretched arms. Too blind to see that the ticket stub in her hand reading "Confused and Hurt — Intensifies With Age," could have read "Paradise — No Expiration Date." The fulfillment of her greatest need was hindered not by the scarcity of God's love, or the difficulty of finding God, but by the depth of her own fear.

The Cross: Saved by the Shame of It All

A frightened kitten and a scared freshmen. Sounds like us sometimes. Desperate times push us to the Light. The teen whose first passing grade occurs on a pregnancy test. The college student whose engagement is called off. The employee whose desk now belongs to someone else. Times like these hit us and we come to the edge of the Light — in need of warmth, acceptance, and spiritual nourishment. We come from the Darkness carrying only burdens and a small ember of hope.

And from the Light a pierced hand reaches out.

What we had hoped for is now reality. Warmth is only a step away. Acceptance is at our fingertips. Yet we doubt. Can he really accept *me*? Dad always said religion was just a crutch. What if he asks too much of me? What if I can't live up to his expectations?

And while the outstretched hand of the Prince of Light reaches into the Darkness and comes closer, we step back — and run. Our hesitancy overcomes our hope. We run back into the blindness and pain of the Darkness from which we were seeking rescue.

For those of you who understand the fear of the unknown, for those of you who have experienced the anxiety of taking the hand of a crucified carpenter, the uncertainty in trusting the One the world renounces — the writer of Hebrews addresses you. In the middle of a text describing the certainty of God's promises, the writer describes those who *have* taken the Hand as people "who have *fled* to take hold of the *hope* offered" (Heb 6:18, italics mine). There is no mixing of words here. There is no skirting around the issue. In simple language the author gives words of comfort to those who are afraid of the Darkness but are unable to trust the Light. Take the Hand. Enter the Light. Don't fear it. Bolt. Fly. Make off. Scamper. Scoot. Skedaddle. Skip. Run to it. Do anything to get to it. Just get to it, and get to it fast.

Why? Because there is hope there. His hands are not empty. The hands of one who has experienced the deepest pains of life have not hardened with age. They have only softened. And this is no plain bowl of milk that he offers. It is the salve for your deepest wounds, the warmth for your coldest fears.

Maybe you've been burned by religion at some point.

Maybe you've been disillusioned with Christianity.

Maybe you learned early on not to trust promises too good to be true.

But this is one promise you can trust. Jesus says that it's worth running for. And he has guaranteed his offer with his own life. Jesus died to prove the certainty of his offer, and now he just wants your hand. He wants you to run. Lay down your fears. Take off your anxieties. Shut your ears to the cries of the world. And run. Run as hard as you can. Take the Hand.

Study Questions

1. What sorts of things have caused you to fear taking the hand of Jesus?

2. In what ways does the cross give you reason to flee to Jesus and take his hand?

3. Is there a sense in which some of our fears of following Jesus are justified?

4. Using the concepts described in this and earlier chapters, how would you convince someone who was afraid of taking the hand that they really should take the hand?

5. Share how your experience as a Christian has helped to prove how groundless some of your earlier fears were.

13

Love's Song
(A Childlike Story)

A long, long time ago, before the stars twinkled, before the mountains touched the sky, there was only the Father, his Spirit, and his Son. Before anything else existed, the Three lived together. They loved each other and spent their time together in the lush gardens of Heaven.

One day as they were walking through the Heavenly gardens, the Three decided that it was time for them to carry out a special plan. It was a plan that they had talked about for a long time. They decided it was time to make the stars, the planets, and humans.

So they began to work. In just six days they created the bright stars, the burning sun, the glowing moon, and the green earth with all its animals and plants. Then the Three sat back in Heaven and looked down on the earth. They were very pleased with what they had made.

With that work done, they began to make man. So they worked very hard again. And at the end of the sixth day, they finished, and they gave man a beautiful garden to live in. They loved man more than anything else they had created.

After they had finished making man, they began to notice that he seemed lonely. So they made a woman to live with him, and the man and woman lived together happily in the garden.

Every day in the shaded garden, as the golden rays of the setting sun danced on the tree leaves, something very special would happen. The Father, his Spirit, and his Son would lean over the delicate clouds in Heaven, and the Father would pick his new children up in his arms. Together the Three would sing this song to the man and the woman:

I love you with a love that began before time,
    And forever more it will burn.
Like a bright fire my love will never die,
    And it will follow you wherever you turn.
This love has made me eternally yours
        and you eternally mine,
    And forever more it will burn.

One day the children were bad and disobeyed the Father. Because of this, the Father had to make them leave the garden. Although he did this, he still loved them very much.

The man and woman eventually had children. Soon they populated the entire earth. Although there were many people on the earth now, every day the Father, his Spirit, and his Son would look down on the people, and at the end of the day they would sing to their children:

I love you with a love that began before time,
    And forever more it will burn.

Like a bright fire my love will never die,
And it will follow you wherever you turn.
This love has made me eternally yours
and you eternally mine,
And forever more it will burn.

Several years passed and more and more people were born. Some of the people were good and listened to the Father and did what he asked them. Others, however, disobeyed the Father and did whatever they wanted. Soon there were more people who disobeyed the Father than there were people who loved him. And even though the Three did good things for the people, the people still disobeyed.

Many people now no longer heard the song of the Three. But every day, as the golden rays of the setting sun danced on the tree leaves and the mountains, the Three would sing their song. Whether the people heard or not, the Three would sing their song of love:

I love you with a love that began before time,
And forever more it will burn.
Like a bright fire my love will never die,
And it will follow you wherever you turn.
This love has made me eternally yours
and you eternally mine,
And forever more it will burn.

Finally the Three decided it was time to carry out another plan. Since the people no longer heard the Heavenly song, one of the Three would go down to the earth and sing the song in person. They had long ago decided that it would be the Son.

So the Son left Heaven and came to earth. He was

born just like any other baby, and lived just like any other man. He wanted to be exactly like the people so that when he sang the song, the people would hear.

Years passed and the Son grew. Finally he decided it was time to sing his song. Many people heard the beautiful song and came to him and asked him about it. The Son told the people about the Father, his Spirit, and himself, and how much they loved them. But some people still didn't hear the song, so the Son continued to sing it wherever he went. For many years the Son sang, trying to tell the people about the Father.

Some of the people who heard the song didn't like it. They became angry with the Son, and they tried to stop him from singing. But their efforts just convinced the Son to sing louder because he loved the people so much. Since the Son wouldn't stop singing, the small group of people who didn't like the song decided they would kill the Son.

One sad day, the people captured the Son and arrested him. They told lies about him to the officials. The next afternoon, the Son was led away to be crucified.

They laid him on a wooden cross and began to nail his hands and feet to the cross. It was painful, especially since the ones killing him were the very ones he loved. The people, filled with hatred, nailed harder and harder, knowing that if they killed the Son, he would never sing the song again.

But as they nailed him and spit on him, the Son began to sing:

I love you with a love that began before time,
> And forever more it will burn.

Like a bright fire my love will never die,
    And it will follow you wherever you turn.
This love has made me eternally yours
        and you eternally mine,
    And forever more it will burn.

They raised the cross and put it in the ground while the words of the song softly floated through the air.

After he finished singing, the Son died, and some friends came and buried him. The Father and his Spirit were very sad, as were some of the people on earth. The people who had done this to the Son were happy and began to celebrate because they thought he would never sing again.

For three days many people cried, including the Father and his Spirit, while the people who had killed the Son celebrated. The air was silent because the sounds of singing could no longer be heard.

Then on the third day, something wonderful happened. In the stillness of the morning, a beautiful sound began to flow out of the stone tomb where the Son had been buried. A few people heard it and began to look for its source. They looked and looked, and finally found where it was coming from. They walked up to the tomb of the Son, and to their surprise, the stone that had covered the entrance was rolled away. They looked inside, but the tomb was empty!

Now the sound no longer seemed to come from the tomb. It seemed to be coming from all around them. As the sounds grew louder, the small group of people began to recognize it. It was the sound of singing! They ran and got some more people and began to look for the source of the singing. After a short time, they found it. There, on a hill rising above the people, stood the Son! He was alive! Although the people had killed him for singing his song, the Son had come back to sing it once more. Tears fell from his eyes, not because he was sad, but because he loved the people so much and wanted them to understand the song.

As he stood in the coolness of the early morning, with the Father and his Spirit looking on, the Son stretched out his arms towards all the people and sang louder and stronger than ever before:

I love you with a love that began before time,
　　And forever more it will burn.
Like a bright fire my love will never die,
　　And it will follow you wherever you turn.
This love has made me eternally yours
　　　　and you eternally mine,
　　And forever more it will burn.

Study Questions

1. Read John 3:16. Explain why other motives besides love (such as wrath, frustration, curiosity) are insufficient to explain why God would send Jesus to the cross.

2. Why do we have such a hard time understanding and appreciating that type of love?

3. If you had lived at the time when Jesus sang this song, do you think you would have listened to it?

4. Explain how that song of love continues through us to other people.

5. Who in your life needs your help in understanding this song of love? What can you do to help them?

✦ 14 ✦

Insincere Pancakes

I'm not sure if it was the quietness of the morning or the rumbling in my stomach that woke me that Saturday. I looked over and the digital clock signaled 7:30 a.m. I had to leave the house early, so I quietly slid out of bed and padded into the kitchen.

I wasn't really hungry that morning — I was ravenous. And as I stood there, swaying side to side and rubbing my sleep filled eyes, my mind took commands from my stomach.

Pancakes! Yes, pancakes! That sounded great. I was tired of cold cereal, and not in the mood for eggs. Pancakes would hit the spot. I could whip up half a recipe for myself in a matter of minutes. I could eat heartily and scoot out of the house before Kendra woke up.

"Chris?" (It was my conscience.)

"Yeah?"

"Shouldn't you also make some for Kendra? You know she would enjoy them."

"Well . . . nah. I'll just cook some up for myself and leave real quick."

"But Chris, you really should fix some for Kendra. She cooked a great supper last night."

"Well . . . nah."

I shoved my conscience aside and went to work.

Let's see, a tablespoon of that. OK, that's done. Oh, that was only supposed to be a teaspoon. Well, I'll just make a little more than half a recipe. I'm pretty hungry anyway.

Two cups of pancake mix. Some milk. Oops! That's too much milk. Better put some more mix in. Oh no, that's too much mix. Now I need more milk, and another egg.

Well, the circus went on in the kitchen for awhile until I had finally managed to make over a full recipe of pancake batter. I didn't want to throw it away, so I decided to cook it. By the end of the ordeal I had at least a dozen pancakes. Much more than even I could handle.

I could freeze them, I thought. Wait! I'll just put them on a plate with some butter and syrup and take them in to Kendra. She'll think I got up early to fix her breakfast in bed and she'll love me for it, and I'll be rid of these extra pancakes.

So I proudly strode into the bedroom with a plate full of pancakes.

"Honey, I made you some breakfast." (Lie.)

Wide eyes full of surprise.

"Here you go."

A big hug and a kiss.

For a moment, as she ate her pancakes in bed, I couldn't have been a better husband in her eyes. To think that I had gotten up early just to make her breakfast in bed. She was astounded.

Then my conscience spoke again.

"You can't get away with this, Chris."

"Sure I can."

"Tell her the truth."

"No."

"Yes."

"No."

"Yes."

Finally I gave in.

Kendra thought she had the first cakes off the grill, when she really only had the leftovers. Her gift came only from the mistake of a selfish husband. Her prince charming was really just a con artist trying to bluff his way out of a bad game.

Have you ever thought about how God gave? The aging apostle John seems to have been considering this when he exclaimed, "How great is the love the Father has lavished on us" (1 John 3:1). Paul told Timothy that "The grace of our Lord was poured out on me abundantly" (1 Tim 1:14). And in his letter to the Roman's, Paul stated it this way: "For if the many died by the trespass of the one man, how much more did God's grace and the gift that came by the grace of the one man, Jesus Christ, overflow to the many!" (Rom 5:15)

Did you catch those wonderful descriptions? Lavished. Poured out. Abundantly. Overflow. Those are not descriptions of something lacking in quantity or quality but of something bursting forth with endless measure. When God decided to give, he didn't hold back. We did not receive some celestial leftover from God's banquet table. We did not receive the small portion of God's treasure that he did not need. We did not receive the fruits of some mistake of God. We received the fullness of all that God could give. He didn't give us a great treasure he owned, or some astounding theory to make life better. He gave us himself in the body of a man. He gave us the very thing which meant the most to him. His Son.

His love was no accident. It was planned before time was invented. And a God who gave like that, will continue to give like that.

Next time you find yourself wanting more than you need, think about that. Next time you're a little down, lift yourself up with that thought. Or next time you find yourself serving insincere pancakes, stop and dwell on God's gift.

Study Questions

1. Who is the "giver" in your family or circle of friends?

2. Would the cross have happened if God measured his giving by the way we often give?

3. In what ways does the cross serve as the only method by which God could exhibit his overflowing love?

4. What areas of your life would be drastically different if you gave as God gave?

5. In what areas of your life have you been giving "insincere pancakes"? What do you need to do to remedy that mistake?

† 15 †

Paradise

The condemned man lay helpless and exhausted as the soldiers sat awkwardly on his outstretched body. Fear pumped heavy beads of sweat onto his sloping forehead. His eyes closed, telling him there was little time left. The rough hand of a soldier tightly gripped his wrist and yanked his arm away from his body. He gasped in fear as he felt the sharp point of an iron spike bending the skin beneath his wrist. He opened his eyes for a second and saw another soldier towering above him like a nightmarish giant with a massive mallet, preparing to bring it down upon the spike resting on his wrist. The mallet fell, hitting its mark, and pain shot from his wrist to his side, and then enveloped his entire body. His back arched as the pain travelled its deadly course.

"Sit still!" barked one of the accompanying soldiers. The comment was punctuated by the back of the soldier's hand raking across his face.

A soldier on his other side grabbed his free wrist and jerked it aside so that his arm was perpendicular to his body. Again he felt the tip of a spike placed against his wrist, and the same hammer was brought down. Goose bumps rose as the hammer fell. Searing pain travelled down his arm as the spike met flesh and travelled through his wrist to the rough timber crossbeam which had become his deathbed.

Shaking uncontrollably, he could feel another soldier grab his feet, pull his legs straight, and cross his feet so that one foot lay on top of the other. The point of a third spike on his foot brought panic to his cloudy mind. Without any warning, it, like the others, was forced through the muscle, bone, and sinews by the force of the soldier's hammer.

This third wave of pain was too great and he slipped into a dead numbness.

"He's done!" shouted a soldier.

"Raise the criminal up!" ordered another.

The criminal felt his body, almost as if it were no longer his, being hoisted up, inch by inch. Darkness fell.

✝

The criminal awoke with a start. He couldn't tell how long he had been unconscious. It felt like a few seconds, but it may have been longer. Now the pain in his wrists and his feet protested too loudly for him to ignore it. Looking left along his narrow arm he saw the head of an iron spike protruding from the bloody flesh of his wrist.

"I can't believe it's going to end like this," he thought. "We didn't make *that* much trouble at the marketplace yesterday. We were just voicing our opinions. I didn't think anyone was really listening anyway, at least no one important. And now I'm going to die! I didn't even want to do it in the first place!"

He looked past the iron spike which had been demanding his attention, past the stranger crucified beside him, and saw his partner hanging on a cross like his. A grimace adorned the partner's face and his body heaved up and down as he tried to breath. Hate filled the criminal's eyes as his partner turned and the two exchanged glances.

"This is your fault!" the criminal wanted to scream. He turned his head from his partner's stare and gazed at the ground below his own feet. He knew it wasn't his partner's fault. He had only himself to blame.

Despite the pain, his mind wandered back to the time when all the trouble had started. He had never really been one to rock the boat. He was by nature a timid and contented person. But there were times when he wished that they could be a free people instead of always living under Rome's shadow. That's when he met a group of people who wanted to do more than just wish. They wanted to act. It sounded exciting and daring, so he spent time with them.

But that was over a year ago. Somehow he got caught up in it all. People were killed. Property was destroyed. And he had managed to suppress what his conscience tried so hard to remind him of. He knew it was wrong from the start. But it brought him a great deal of satisfaction, and he had lots of friends now, and . . .

"Now . . . now I'll be dead in a matter of hours," he thought.

His thoughts were interrupted as his ears caught the sound of a ladder being tossed against wood. He turned his head and saw a soldier climbing up a ladder on the cross next to his. The soldier, dressed in thick military leather, carried a grin on his face and a piece of wood in his hand. The criminal noticed writing on the piece of wood, but he couldn't make it out.

When the soldier reached the top of the ladder, he faced the man crucified on the cross between the two criminals.

"Sorry, *King*," he said sarcastically. "We forgot to put your royal title up."

As the criminal watched, the soldier nailed the piece of wood above the head of the man crucified there. The soldier finished and climbed down the ladder, laughing. Straining his head to see the writing on the wood, the criminal could just barely make out a few words on the bottom of the sign.

King . . . of . . . the . . . Jews. King of the Jews? Who *was* this person? King of the Jews. He thought back to a time when he and his grandfather had gone to the temple. Its size still made him feel like an ant. The next week they went to the synagogue. He was a Jew by birth, but he hadn't practiced any of the religion until his gray-haired grandfather took him to the synagogue. He remembered how boring he thought it would be. But it wasn't. The stories of what God had done were hard to believe, but the more he heard, the more he wanted to know. He had been so eager to learn and to get involved in his Jewish heritage.

But that was before he met his partner. Now he

would definitely know more. But with life near its end, he wished he could change things. He wished he could have really known God. But it was too late. There was no chance of that now.

Below him a wave of laughter washed through the crowd that had gathered at the crucifixion site. He looked down and saw a few of the soldiers laughing at the man crucified next to him.

Poor man, he thought. He's suffered the crucifixion, and now this. Why don't they leave him alone?

"Father, forgive them, for they do not know what they are doing."

The criminal couldn't believe the words which had just come from the man's mouth.

Father?! *Forgive* them?! As far as he was concerned those soldiers and that crowd could just join him on the cross today. *Forgive* them! King of the Jews? Who was this man?

"Come down from the cross, *if* you are the Son of God!"

Son of God? Father? A thought began to materialize in the criminal's slow mind and a vague memory was stirred. This must be the one I've heard about. *Jesus*! This guy must be Jesus! Even he had heard the rumors of the healings, miracles, and bold claims of this man Jesus. He and his partner's escapades against establishment held nothing to this man Jesus. But he had never seem him before.

The criminal looked again at the man crucified beside him. The pain began to throb in his arms now. Breathing was accompanied by the screams of every nerve in his body. But he ignored the pain and looked hard at Jesus.

The Son of God — could it be?

As he thought, he glanced downward again. The crowd had grown larger now, and all their attention seemed to be focused on the one crucified next to him, on Jesus.

Why all the attention? Why all the harsh cries? Why all the hate? Even the men dressed ornately in robes spewed words of hate towards this man.

The criminal looked back at Jesus. The air hung heavy with evil words, yet this man said not even a single word in revenge. In fact, as the criminal looked closer, he thought he saw tears lingering in the corners of Jesus' eyes. Tears not of hate, but of love.

Could he really be the one he claimed to be? He had never thought much of all those rumors and arguments about this man from . . . where was it? Nazareth?! Yet now, with three nails holding him over the abyss of death, things seemed different. And this man Jesus was not acting the way a normal person should. Either Jesus was crazy, or . . .

It was hard for the criminal to finish the thought.

He studied Jesus intently. Again, the pain swept through his body like a hurricane. But he swallowed hard and forced himself to think.

Looking at Jesus, the criminal noted that he was like any man on the street. His curly brown hair dripped from the sweat of pain. His sun-bronzed face showed the effects of a working life. Yet, his eyes. There was something about his eyes. They were so . . . honest.

He didn't know why, but he was beginning to believe in this man. Though everyone else in the crowd below seemed to oppose Jesus, the criminal felt a burning in his heart he had never felt before.

Yet just as a flicker of hope and joy began to dance within his crumbling heart, it was engulfed by despair and the harsh reality of the situation.

I am a *criminal!* A *criminal!* I *had* my chance, but I chose *this*. I could have followed the God of my fathers, but I *chose* this. It makes no difference if this man crucified next to me really is the Son of God. I have chosen my path and now I must pay. Nothing can change that. Nothing!

The pain of the nails hit him again, along with the thoughts of the hopelessness of the situation. Tears of suffering and despair flooded his eyes, pouring as they never had before.

"It is too late for me!" he thought. "It is *too late!!*"

As he struggled with the fear and the regrets, he heard a familiar voice. It was the voice of his partner crucified on the other side of Jesus.

"Aren't *you* the *Christ?!* Save yourself, and *us!*"

The voice was filled with hatred and desperation, and was void of the remorse which the criminal had been feeling. The emotion of these final hours provoked undisciplined thoughts and words from his partner.

And while thinking came hard, there was a feeling deep inside the criminal that said, "These mobs are wrong. This man is different!"

His partner had reacted in anger and defiance, but something in the criminal's heart told him his partner was as wrong facing death as he had been in living life.

Then the burning in his heart began again.

This man is *not* a liar, he really *is* the Christ! Even though it may be too late for me, at least I can end my life doing something right for once.

With deep resolve, the criminal painfully forced himself upright. He felt the muscles in his feet tear and he groaned with pain. As he straightened out, he took a deep breath, and spoke the truest message he had ever spoken. He tried to inhale deeply, and his raspy breath ushered out valiant words.

"Don't you fear God, since you are under the same sentence?"

He took another deep breath while his body protested.

"We are punished justly, for we are getting what our deeds deserve."

Another breath was taken, and the air burned in his lungs as he spoke.

"But *this* man has done *nothing* wrong!"

Even as the last words left his sun-cracked lips, he could hardly believe he had said them. Before he could think any more about the depth of what he had just confessed, Jesus raised his head, placing it between the criminal's stare and his partner. Pain was evident in his face, and it seemed to torture him to turn to meet the criminal face to face.

The criminal, facing the one he had so boldly defended, was now deeply ashamed. He lowered his eyes as Jesus faced him from his cross.

"If this man is truly the Son of God, then he knows who I am. He knows what I've done and that I deserve to be here. If it is true, then he has the power to condemn me, and he has every right to do so," the criminal thought.

Yet he felt a newfound courage rising within him, and against his will, he looked upward and met the eyes of Jesus. Though no words left Jesus' mouth, his eyes spoke a deep appreciation to the criminal.

"He thanked me! He knows who I am and what I've done, and he thanked me! The Son of God thanked me! Maybe there *is* hope for me!" He thought about the significance of what had just happened, and as he did, he began to push the envelope of his thinking even further.

I wonder if this Jesus would grant me forgiveness? Though he knew it was a senseless thought, still he wanted to know. "He seems so kind," he thought. Even facing death there was a peacefulness about him. The criminal wanted to ask Jesus for mercy, for forgiveness, and his heart urged "Ask him, Ask him." "What do I have to lose?" he thought.

The criminal swallowed hard, and one last time struggled for breath, for enough air to allow him to speak, and acted with his heart. As he forced the air over dry and swollen vocal chords, the boldest request ever to come from his heart fell from his parched lips.

"Jesus, remember me . . ."

Halfway through the statement he began to lower his eyes. He could not face Jesus as he stated his request.

". . . when you come into your kingdom."

As he finished, he looked back up at Jesus, half expecting to be met with eyes full of disbelief or condemnation. Yet the same eyes that met him earlier met him now. Eyes full of love and compassion.

Suddenly, the slight breeze that had been blowing stopped. It seemed that all the noise from the crowd ceased as if the crowd had been cleared away. But the criminal didn't look below to see. He was transfixed by the gaze of this man called Jesus.

He wanted to say more, to say how sorry he was for all he had done, to cry, to say he could have done better. And yet he felt strangely as if he already had.

"If I could just have the smallest blessing from this man," he thought, "I would be more than satisfied."

Then the doubts began to rise in his mind. "What have I just asked? I deserve to die. I deserve nothing from Jesus. Why should *I* be forgiven?"

The thoughts began to flow faster and faster, cascading into another flood of despair. But just before their peak, just before their flow became unbearable, the stream was broken by a small sound.

It was Jesus taking a breath.

The criminal turned once more and met the eyes of Jesus. Jesus looked as if he were going to say something.

"Oh no," thought the criminal. "Here it comes. I should have just kept quiet. Now I will hear what I have known all along. I deserve no mercy, especially from the Son of God."

Jesus, seeming to sense the man's fear, bent his head closer to the criminal's. The crown of thorns forced fresh drops of blood over his eyes and blurred his vision. But his voice was clear — weak and filled with emotion, but clear. Then Jesus whispered the most wonderful words the criminal would ever hear:

"I tell you the truth, today you *will* be with me in Paradise."

Have you ever heard a more absurd story? One who has spent the last portion of his life violently opposing authority and taking from others is given the best that God can give. How could God forgive someone like that? And even more puzzling, how could God give him that which others would have died to possess? This criminal didn't even have time to clean up his act, to do something bold and spiritual with his life to show his repentance. Paradise! As far as we know he didn't do a single thing for God his whole life, and he was given Paradise!

While this man hung in punishment for the crimes he committed, God hung next to him simultaneously taking that man's punishment on himself. As each second slipped by, the criminal came closer to death. But he also came that much closer toward a loving God. As he smelled the putrid odor of the wrongness of his life, the grace of God filled his nostrils.

Some may think that this man just squeaked in as the gates of Hope began to swing shut. But I think they were open the whole time.

What do you suppose God did the day this criminal was born? I can't say for sure, but I think that as the infant criminal-to-be dropped into his mother's arms, God smiled. Oh sure, God knew what kind of person this man would turn out to be. He knew about the rebellion, the stealing, the hiding. This man would be no great moral example, and would not stand strong for the Lord.

The Cross: Saved by the Shame of It All

But I think on that morning God had to smile. He knew what was in store for this man. God was going to shock his socks off. God would watch and wait. He would watch this man speak his first words in favor of vehement rebellion. He would watch him take part in his first riot. And He would wait. And just as the criminal had lost all hope, just when there was no light left, he would lean over to his tired ear and whisper; "You know what? I know you. I know what you've done and who you are. But you want to know a secret? I love you." I think God smiled as he thought of that moment. The gates of Heaven would open wide for this dirty criminal.

All he could do was weakly profess his newfound belief in Jesus and sorrowfully confess the wreck he had made of his life. And I guess in God's eyes, that was enough. That was all it took. Even on a Roman cross, hours from death, that's all it took. In that instant, his entire past was erased, and his entire future was ensured, by a God who hung next to him. This criminal stands as a reminder that God knows us the best, and even with that knowledge, he loves us the most. That love compels him to say to all who will listen, "Today, you will be with me in Paradise."

Study Questions

1. Read Luke 23:26-43. Explain the difference between the disgrace the criminal faced on the cross and the disgrace Jesus faced on the cross.

2. If you had been hanging on the cross next to Jesus, what would have been harder for you to believe: that this really was the Son of God, or that he might forgive you?

3. How could Jesus forgive this criminal without also seeing if he would "take up his cross and follow me"?

4. What differentiated this criminal from his partner that would compel Jesus to forgive him?

5. Why does this story *not* support the idea that we should just live any way we want and then plan to have a "deathbed conversion" like this criminal so that we get into heaven?

⌗16⌗

Speeding Tickets*

It was just another steamy summer day in Memphis. The clock on the wall said it was a quarter to five, so I grabbed my keys and wallet, and ran out the door. In fifteen minutes my wife would be finishing work.

I drove through some side streets and wound my way up to Poplar, one of the main streets that would take me all the way to the two-storied brick building where Kendra worked. As I turned onto the six lane street, I popped in a tape and slid the car into fifth gear, gliding along with the rest of the traffic.

40 . . . 45 . . . 50 . . .

Hmmm, I wonder what's going on up there? Must be some construction work — there's a guy standing in the middle of my lane. What's he doing? Oh, he's waving me over. Must be a detour. Wait a minute — construction worker's don't wear black. Oh no! It's a cop!

---

*"Speeding Tickets" first appeared in *Wineskins* 2:2 (1993).

And one of Memphis's finest pulled me over to a side street beside his imposing motorcycle.

"Clocked you doing 52 in a 40 m.p.h. zone."

"I didn't know that it was only 40. You see, I'm sorta new here, only been here a month or so and . . . ."

"Let me see your license."

"But you see . . . ," as I pulled out my license.

"Address?"

"Well, it's like this . . . ," as I grunted out my address.

"Ok, sign here. You can pay sixty-one dollars at this address here, or you can pay thirty-four dollars if you want it to go on your record."

Silently I was begging him for mercy, for some sign of compassion, but none came through his black sunglasses.

"Here you go. Have a nice day."

Have a nice day?! Boy, I couldn't wait to show this to my wife. Thirty four dollars! And even then it would go on my record.

Several weeks after that incident, I still find myself being overly cautious as I drive the same road to pick up Kendra. I drive it much differently than I used to. Now I let the orange arm of the speedometer barely touch the outer point of 40 and no more. Cars zip past me in the other two lanes, but I don't budge. I drive a very safe forty. I've learned my lesson.

It's interesting to reflect on why I drive the way I now do. Before, I would drive whatever speed everyone else was driving. If they drove forty, so would I. If they drove fifty, so would I. Now I just drive forty, period.

Do I drive forty because I have come to sincerely

respect the officer's wish for me to drive slower? Probably not. Do I drive forty because I want to show my love and appreciation for the city of Memphis and the state of Tennessee? Probably not. I drive forty for one simple reason: I don't want to get caught again. I can't afford it.

This kind of motivation is easy to understand. It's an attitude of survival. We learn it from the time we are little.

"Don't hit your sister again, or you'll regret it."

"If you say one more word, you're going to get it."

"Remember what happened last time you wouldn't listen to me?!"

It's the reason many of us get to work on time in the morning. It's the reason we try to file our income tax returns before that April 15 deadline. Over the course of our lives we learn an ever present rule: Do bad and get punished, do good and avoid punishment. Very simple. Very straightforward. And it works — for awhile.

It works until we meet a God who would say good-bye to his only Son. It works until we come face to face with a Savior who is dying to embrace us. It works until we read the boldface letters on the Deed of Salvation: Debt paid in full (see Grace). And God changes the rule.

Do we deserve punishment? You bet. Did we mess up? More than we can know. But do we get punished? No. God took care of that side of the equation. On a dark afternoon in Palestine God took care of that.

But some of us still try to live as if He didn't. Even some of us who follow the Master still live as if that shabby rule is true. We take care of our neighbor. We

197

read our Bible. We go to church. But only to avoid punishment. Some of us live our lives as I have learned to drive my car. We obey the "rules" only to avoid punishment. The result? Peace is a running river we try to grasp but can't. Joy is a stranger we have never met. And God is an imposing man behind dark sunglasses, waiting to give speeding tickets. The promise of the Savior that we would find rest for our souls seems to us an empty one.

I think God knows we tend to work that way. Maybe that's why he created an earthly Paradise for man and woman before talking about rules. Perhaps that's why he led a band of sandled slaves across a dry sea bed in Egypt before he gave them the law. Perhaps that's why he met death before meeting you and me. Not to butter us up. Not to make us feel obligated. But to make us feel loved. To help us see that no matter what we may have done in the past, he can secure our future.

Paul's summary of the work of the Incarnate says it best: "For the wages of sin is death, but the gift of God is eternal life in Christ Jesus our Lord (Rom 6:23)." Christianity is not desperate deeds done by one to avoid the fiery wrath of God. It is the natural acts of love that come from one who deserves nothing but has been given everything. With the exclamation point of the cross, God has called us. Not to condemn our past and make the present a joyless burden, but to secure our future and make the present abundantly joyful.

Study Questions

1. Share some things you do each week because you're afraid of being caught by someone if you don't do them.

2. What is the difference between doing religious things to avoid the wrath of God, and doing them because we already have the love of God?

3. What motivation, fear of wrath or gratitude for love, has been the primary motivator in your walk with God? What can you do to be more motivated by gratitude?

4. Is there a place for fear in our walk with God? Explain.

5. How can the cross help motivate you toward even more sacrificial service to God?

Chris Altrock is Jordan's father and Kendra's husband. His life has been changed by the cross and he hopes yours will too. He loves preaching and writing about the cross and the One who died upon it. The University Church of Christ in Las Cruces, New Mexico, gives him the privilege of talking about Jesus every Sunday. When he's not preaching, writing, father-ing, or husband-ing, he enjoys serving the children of Las Cruces through the Full Speed Ahead ministry and travels regularly into Mexico to serve churches and children there.